PRAISE FOR MOLLIE PAINTON
and *Encouraging Your Child's Spiritual Intelligence*

"Anyone interested in the spirituality of children must read *Encouraging Your Child's Spiritual Intelligence*. While I thoroughly enjoyed this unique and heartfelt book, I was captivated by the fascinating stories Mollie tells as she introduces us to children on each branch of the Spiritual Tree of Life. She teaches us to respect, support, and interact with these spiritual children in order to strengthen their gifts and self-esteem. At moments I found myself experiencing a newfound joy as I rediscovered my own forgotten spiritual child within. Her exhaustive resource section of movies, books, magazines, and support groups further enhanced my understanding and acceptance of spiritual intelligence that should be added to Gardner's list of multiple intelligences."

—**Cathie McCallum**, B.S., Early Childhood Education;
M.A., Guidance and Counseling;
college instructor in Early Childhood Education

"The world is a better place because Mollie Painton poured her soul into every page of *Encouraging Your Child's Spiritual Intelligence*."

—**Hugh Prather**, minister and author of *Notes to Myself*,
Spiritual Parenting, and *Morning Notes*

"I found *Encouraging Your Child's Spiritual Intelligence* to be unique both in content and approach. Mollie's years of working with children affords her special insight into their emotional, psychological, and spiritual realms. The children's stories that she shares help to remind us that we too are spiritual beings and encourage us to pay attention to what is a vivid part of children's lives and our lives as well, full of insight and wisdom. The seven branches of spiritual intelligence that Mollie so clearly describes are a useful tool in identifying a spiritually gifted child. After fifteen years of working as a counselor in a hospice setting, I especially appreciate the attention Mollie gives to the third and fourth branches, Physical Death and A World of Spirit. Children and adults alike seem to have a particular openness to this aspect of their inner life when in the midst of grief. It is at times of loss or crisis that children may most benefit from the presence of a sensitive and supportive spiritual partner. This will be a book we will include in our hospice library to be read by parents and other adult caregivers."

—**Nancy Jakobsson**, LCSW, director of Pathways: Programs for Grief and Loss

"This book is filled with rich and surprising firsthand accounts of the inner world of children. These compelling descriptions of compassion and wisdom, credible otherworldly encounters, healing, and awareness add significantly to the growing body of evidence that children do indeed have rich and remarkable spiritual lives. Beyond helping the reader recognize children's natural and varied spiritual intelligence, these stories engender the remembrance of our own spiritual capacities while providing grounded suggestions for becoming spiritual allies to our children."

—**Tobin Hart**, Ph.D., licensed psychologist; Associate Professor of Psychology at the State University of West Georgia; founder of the Child/Spirit Institute; author of *The Secret Spiritual World of Children* and other books

"In this very readable book, Mollie Painton has done us all a great service by alerting us and sensitizing us to the revelation that comes to us from God through the children's stories she shares and through her experienced reflections on their stories. The first invitation is to awaken to this largely ignored source of spiritual nourishment. The second invitation is to awaken to our role to be humble, caring, and sensitive spiritual companions to the children in our lives. You will be enriched by Mollie's book and by saying 'yes' to these two invitations. Thank you, Mollie!"

—**Jim Reid**, M.Th., M.A., LCSW, religious education director at Blessed John the XXIII Catholic University Center and a psychotherapist in private practice

Encouraging Your Child's
Spiritual Intelligence

ENCOURAGING YOUR CHILD'S
Spiritual Intelligence

MOLLIE PAINTON, PSY.D.

ATRIA BOOKS
New York London Toronto Sydney

BEYOND WORDS
PUBLISHING

ATRIA BOOKS
1230 Avenue of the Americas
New York, N.Y. 10020

BEYOND WORDS
PUBLISHING
20827 N.W. Cornell Road, Suite 500
Hillsboro, Oregon 97124-9808
503-531-8700
503-531-8773 fax
www.beyondword.com

Editor: Sue Mann
Managing editor: Henry Covi
Copyediting/proofreading: Marvin Moore
Cover and interior design: Carol Sibley
Composition: William H. Brunson Typography Services

Manufactured in the United States of America

Library of Congress Cataloging-in-Publication Data
Painton, Mollie.
    Encouraging your child's spiritual intelligence / by Mollie Painton.
        p. cm.
    Includes bibliographical references and index.
    1. Children—Religious life.   2. Healing—Religious aspects.   3. Play therapy.   I. Title.
    BL625.5.P35   2006
    618.92′891653—dc22

                                        2006023906

ISBN-13: 978-1-58270-149-3
ISBN-10:   1-58270-149-0

First Atria Books / Beyond Words trade paperback edition January 2007

10 9 8 7 6 5 4 3 2 1

The corporate mission of Beyond Words Publishing, Inc.: *Inspire to Integrity*

*For my own spiritual children, Daniel, Sarah, and Cathleen, along
with spiritual children of all ages*

*For Max, my husband, whose short life gifted his children
and me with the beginnings of this book*

For my sister, Mary Jan, who was undoubtedly a spiritual child

Contents

Preface

My Story

In 1979 my husband, Max, died, leaving me with two daughters, ages three and seven. Although I was devastated by my loss and aware of my daughters' pain, their wisdom and openness touched me.

For the first few years both of our daughters verbalized their distress as they grieved the loss of their father. However, they seemed comforted that Max visited them often. Some encounters were in dreams; others were face-to-face. Rather than frightening them, the visits were usually heartwarming, even at times entertaining. They loved keeping alive the connection with their father.

Their experiences reminded me of a visitor I had a few months before Max died. In the middle of the night I woke. Standing next to my bed was an incredible being. The figure appeared Christlike, with a yellowish light permeating him and a veil draped over his body, including his head. The entire room took on a soft glow from his presence. Although he did not speak, I felt his tremendous power— an energy I believed was born of his unfathomable compassion. Without his uttering a sound, I felt his infinite love and that I was completely safe in his hands.

In the morning Max and I looked at each other with astonishment. I told him that a Christlike figure had appeared to me. He said, "Well, an angel came to me!" We never said another word about this to each other. We never disclosed any details, nor did we question, "What really had happened that night? Who was the man whose appearance was Christlike? Who was Max's angel?" As far as I know, neither of us told anyone else that this had happened, until nearly ten years later, long after Max's death, when I told this story to my daughters.

I had always been intrigued with psychology. (I read Carl Menninger's *The Human Mind* from cover to cover when I was thirteen years old.) When I decided to get my doctorate, I chose to work therapeutically with girls and boys who were still highly imaginative, creative, and spiritually open. I was compelled to learn all I could from these incredibly knowing children. I realize now I had wanted, perhaps needed, to reclaim those sensitive parts of myself that I had abandoned.

These astonishing children shared with me their compassionate wisdom, gifts, and innocence—extraordinary resources at their disposal for healing, survival, and enrichment. By seeing that which is normally not seen, they were better prepared to live in a world that often was hurtful to them. Ultimately, they taught me to be at peace with my remarkable experiences, to enjoy those encounters as spiritual resources rather than as personal liabilities.

What You Will Gain

I believe that all of us as children enjoyed spiritual doors which were wide open—or at least slightly ajar. Most of us were not encouraged to preserve these gifts. However, our children needn't suffer as we did.

Within these children's stories you will find yourself—as well as your children. Your awareness of the spiritual life of these children will greatly soften your world as you become able to easily tune in to their presence. You'll feel their uniqueness as wonderful rather than confusing and disheartening. Your acquaintance with these children will allow you to better understand your own qualities related to the spiritual child who lives within you and who is awaiting the opportunity to be a spiritual partner. At the same time you'll learn to identify, nurture, and protect not only obviously spiritual children but also those who have tremendous potential while not demonstrating spiritual characteristics.

Indeed, this book is a treasure hunt for all who are seeking to reclaim their spiritual child within while encouraging the spiritual intelligence of children in their care. Let these kids expand your horizons, as they have mine. Learn how to identify and enhance the spiritual world of children and emerge with a sense of peace, hope, and love along with the rediscovery of your own precious gifts.

Acknowledgments

Recently I was touched by the presence of an enormous golden eagle that flew straight across my path as I drove down a mountain highway in Colorado. I gasped as its massive body blocked the view of the entire windshield while its vast wing covered the top of the car. Dazed by the eagle's elegance, I felt a deep gratitude for the blessings that my connection with nature has continuously bestowed upon me.

I was also filled with a sense of awakened thankfulness to so many adult spiritual children who have supported me for over a decade as I poured heart and soul into this book. To these dear friends I offer my deepest appreciation: Elke Calmes, whose depth and courage have helped me to always look at the more profound meaning of life and with whom I can share my love of nature; Mary Parker, whose true friendship for over forty years has taught me the power of hope and forgiveness; Kathy Corso, who has always been there for me with an open heart and home; and Pat Lape, whose love and encouragement have inspired me to enjoy life and "keep an eye open for what magic might be around the next corner." Many others remain unnamed but nonetheless are greatly treasured.

Acknowledgments

To a number of extraordinary educators and friends—Byron and Carol Norton, George Tate, Judith Praul, Carol Lutey, the Catholic Sisters of Divine Providence Patrice and Charlene, Bill Hillman, Vaughn Huff, Janet Fritz, and Tobin and Mary Hart—I wish to express my deepest gratitude for combining caring, inspiration, understanding, and warmth with teaching, insight, and knowledge.

To the multicultural communities with whom I have interacted, I am forever grateful for sharing with me their beliefs in the unseen, along with their spirit of true brotherhood/sisterhood and hospitality.

Special heartfelt thanks to Cathy Simmering, whose unwavering faith in me has nurtured my own spiritual child within and made this book possible; and to Scott Tate, whose incredible gift of guiding others through dark times has sustained me during mine.

To my publisher, Cynthia Black, who has great capacity for vision and is dauntless in her mission to offer the world inspiration and insight, I offer my deepest appreciation.

To my parents, who were steadfast in providing me with a religious background from which my spiritual life flowered, I thank from the bottom of my heart; to my siblings, who filled my childhood with delightful companionship and an opportunity to mutually share our spiritual worlds, I wish to express my gratitude.

To my three children, Cathleen, Sarah, and Daniel, my most meaningful, enjoyable, and rewarding works of love, who have taught me more than I could ever share, I extend my arms in a gesture of support and encouragement as they choose to play, work, and grow on all seven branches of the Spiritual Tree of Life.

To Max, I do not have the words to say how much you are missed, loved, and appreciated. Your spirit has thrust me forward on my journey. Your presence is felt.

Finally, it is with tears of joy as a lost soul who has found her way home that I offer my deepest appreciation and encouragement to all the spiritual children, of all ages, whose paths I have been so blessed to cross. Their wisdom, compassion, journeys of rebirth, and spiritual play have enriched my life, as I am sure they will yours.

Introduction

A World of Possibilities and Dreams

Looking back over my years of working with children, I realize that despite the fact that I was not embracing my own spirituality, there was a certain innocence and openness about me that made children feel it was safe to tell me nearly anything. They were not afraid I would judge, criticize, or reject them. Thus, they shared experiences they were not comfortable disclosing to others. These stories, whether played out or spoken, gently challenged me to let go of my need for logic and scientific proof, to honestly confront my rigid perspective while I was gradually molded into a true protector, a confidante, and a source of strength for them.

Although I helped these boys and girls to safely express their trauma, losses, and pain, they gradually awakened in me the slumbering spiritual giant of my childhood. As they found a sense of spiritual kinship and belonging in their playful relationships with me, they continued to invite me to be a privileged visitor in their world of the invisible. Blessed by the deep trust inherent in their invitation, I felt that I, at the same time, was liberated from the confinement of my narrow beliefs. My own spiritual intelligence was awakened, and to this day I enjoy great freedom in realizing a much richer world of possibilities and dreams. In this process, I learned how to accompany these children on their journeys as a spiritual partner.

Spiritual Children

Working with the parents of spiritually gifted kids, I have often alleviated fears about their children by making them aware of the term *spiritual intelligence* in relation to their children's unique needs and characteristics. When they understand who their children are from such a positive and hopeful perspective, parents usually believe they can respond in a helpful manner. Sometimes a parent has been effective in educating a teacher, neighbor, or counselor about the child having a special set of skills and needs. When this concept is understood, no longer will spiritually gifted children suffer from the stigma of more severe—and often inaccurate—diagnoses and assessments that can lead to adults' fear-based and judgmental responses. Both adults and children will enjoy greater freedom as they pursue opportunities to evolve in a constructive way based on a perspective of giftedness as opposed to handicaps.

Dozens of parents have responded with relief and even exuberance when I suggested that they, too, are spiritually gifted children. None refused to believe this statement; they realized it was an amazing truth they had known on some level for years but were unable to verbalize. They never had the opportunity to recognize or validate themselves in this light—or perhaps they never had the awareness that spiritual intelligence, such as they had experienced, existed.

You may ask, "Are all children spiritual? Was I a spiritually gifted child?" All children occupy a unique place on the continuum labeled *spiritual intelligence.* Some are sensitive, wise, and compassionate peacemakers or are powerful healers. Others are privy to a variety of gifts and experiences, such as contact with deceased loved ones, visiting invisible worlds, seeing lights around people, having near-death experiences, desiring to fly while remembering the freedom to do so, and predicting the future with profound insight or intuition, awake or in dreams. Some kids are high on the spirituality continuum; many show no reportable signs of being a spiritual child.

Wise people from nearly every culture believe that contacting hidden realities and communicating with spirits are natural occurrences. For instance, while playing hide-and-go-seek at dusk with his siblings and cousins, a boy in the Philippines saw a ghostlike female figure on the staircase of his home. When he told his family, his grandmother pulled out the picture album and asked him to identify the woman. He readily found the person, clothing included, whom he had seen. His parents and grandmother smiled knowingly. Because his experience was believed, respected, and not considered out of the ordinary, he derived a sense of validation and importance as a spiritual child.

Regrettably, spiritually intelligent kids in the West often find themselves lost in a world that does not believe or support, much less nurture, their gifts. To the scientific materialistic mind of the Westerner, seeing is believing. It is confusing to most persons influenced purely by the Western mind to grasp that children encounter realities that cannot be seen by the ordinary eye. That which is unseen or unable to be measured is inconceivable.

It is difficult, at best, for children confronted with the Westerner's scientific mind to feel they are valued as the precious spiritual beings they are. Thus, spiritual kids have good cause to fear rejection based on adults' comments and destructive behaviors. In his article "Adults Who Had Imaginary Playmates as Children" (from the book *Mental Imagery* by Robert Kunzendorf), John Connolly relates a boy's story:

> *I have a twelve-year-old cousin who had an imaginary friend when he was smaller. It drove his father crazy. One day his dad had had enough of it and asked him where his friend BoBo was, and when he pointed it out, my uncle stomped down as hard as he could and smashed BoBo into the ground. My cousin turned pale and wouldn't talk for the rest of the day. That is how he lost his imaginary friend.*[1]

Spiritual Partnership

Children in today's world are hungering for a nurturing relationship with a spiritual partner. After years of envisioning this adult role as one of guardian, mentor, teacher, guide, or guru, I now realize that the backing spiritual kids need while on their journeys is from spiritual partners, people who will provide a mutual exchange of information along with recognition, nurturance, validation, and protection. The term *mutual* implies a reciprocal, equal, and shared process, whereas *guardian* implies that the adult is in a superior or dominant role to the child rather than accompanying the child on a give-and-take journey of knowing, learning, and growing.

I believe that every child has at least a modicum of spiritual intelligence. I believe that every child may blossom in varying degrees if accompanied by a spiritual partner. Fortunately, some children retain a good portion of their giftedness even if they are not given the support they need. However, these kids are unusual, perhaps extraordinarily gifted, more spiritually tenacious, and strongly grounded by nature (as opposed to nurture) than others. Although they maintain many open doors to their spiritual world despite a lack of encouragement, they may still suffer by not being able to develop their potential as fully as they would with support. These children are strong of heart, but they may endure some confusion and poor self-esteem along with a sense that they are so different something must be wrong with them. With recognition, nurturance, and protection, they will eventually discover themselves to be greater, more gifted persons than they had ever dreamed possible.

Without the help and acceptance of spiritual partners, however, most children will gradually forsake their inner spiritual worlds. Unfortunate as it would be for an adult to die this kind of spiritual death, it is an unforgivable tragedy for children to feel it is necessary to seal off the richness of their inner world in order to live. When they begin to lose access to their inner sanctum, many doors to awareness will close and their gifts will be lost. For a child this is a spiritual death that sets in motion a cycle of suffering that may last a lifetime.

The subtle skill of encouraging children to develop their creative gifts of music and art is closely related to the work of a spiritual partner. For instance, one mother remembers being told by her music teacher that she normally would discourage her ability to be a concert pianist because of the small size of her hands. However, the teacher believed she would always excel with the piano because of her deep soul connection to the music as well as to the world. A father told of his grandfather who encouraged art when the father was a child, pointing out all the beauty and color in the nature of the countryside. As insignificant as these interactions may seem, they were unforgettable, life-changing statements that validated these children's lives as related to the soul. At the same time, these declarations were invaluable seeds that when planted and nourished may have led to the blossoming of the children's creative, if not spiritual, potential.

You may ask, "Who, indeed, is the teacher in this relationship?" Usually, spiritually intelligent children are wise and compassionate beings who have great reservoirs of spiritual gifts, characteristics, and experiences. Although adults have far too often closed the door to their spiritual lives, children are giants in their openness to this fascinating world. Adults necessarily assume a position of authority when teaching, structuring, and disciplining their children; spiritual partnership, however, compels all participants to inhabit a common ground.

So, why do our children so desperately need us to be their spiritual partners? As adults, we have the capacity to help children feel comfortable in their spirituality or decide to abandon their gifts and close their spiritual door. We can also make sure they feel safe by offering validation without question and by protecting them from a world that too often is critical of, even at times threatening to, their spirituality. Don't forget that as spiritual partners we also need support, validation, and encouragement as we don many hats; we learn to enrich our relationship with our children by sharing anecdotes that describe our struggle to survive with our unique gifts. Fortunately for us, as adults in partnership with spiritual children, we are likely to benefit by allowing our own spirituality once again, or even for the first time, to blossom.

Becoming a spiritual partner is the work of a lifetime and cannot be accomplished in isolation. After reading this book, joining an adult support group could help you to further explore such questions as these: "Am I a wise and compassionate spiritual partner to my child? (*My child* is defined here as any influential relationship with a child as a son or daughter, student, client, Sunday school participant, patient, and more.) If not, what must I do to achieve a mutually gratifying partnership? Is my child a spiritual child? Or, with my help, does my child have the potential to become a spiritual child?"

The Spiritual Tree of Life

Spiritually gifted children have a natural wisdom that enables them to live an enriched life unexplained by the physical properties of science and beyond the confines of rationalism. They are wise and compassionate healers who are deeply purposeful, driven by their heartfelt desire to connect with all people while mending the wounds of loss, judgment, abuse, hate, indifference, disease, and violence. Predominantly influenced by their sacred God-given gifts, these boys and girls are on journeys of personal and communal growth.

In their wisdom they are very aware of the constant presence of good and evil, of light and darkness. They have demonstrated this knowledge in their play as spiritual warriors. Although the scenarios vary in intensity and length, nearly every spiritual child was involved, at least to some degree, in these confrontations. Many of these kids also taught me that death is permanent only in a physical sense. They made me aware of the beauty, power, and expressiveness of metaphor and healing play, that they live in a world composed primarily of spirit, and that many of them experience transformation— shedding their old lives on the road to spiritual rebirth—as a place of both joy and sorrow. As I studied their behaviors, thoughts, feelings, healing play, intentions, trauma, wisdom, compassion, and caring connection, I was struck by the universal characteristics and themes that continually repeated themselves in each child.

After so many years of close contact with spiritual children, my consciousness was expanding in all directions. I found myself in a fresh, vast, and astonishing world—the world of the spiritual child. In the center of their incredible world I visualized a grand, playful, and childlike tree that stood with great presence. Its trunk was both massive and sturdy, providing support to the interconnected network of seven major branches. And as I envisioned this astonishing tree that welcomes all children to play on its branches, the name *Spiritual Tree of Life* came to me.

I know that the image of the Tree of Life is so rich it is referred to in the Kabbalah and the Bible. In the context of my book it is a life-giving tree with seven major branches of spirituality that children have brought to my awareness. The greater the spiritual intelligence, the more comprehensive access boys and girls have to the many branches.

This tree sways courageously with the sometimes not-so-gentle wind of transformation. As it protects children during their storms, they find within its branches the fruits of spiritual life: unity, harmony, and balance. After the storm, when the tree opens its canopy to the light, children playing on its seven branches, as well as their personal and global families, are drenched in the sunlight of enrichment, expansion, and a deepened inner life.

As modern-day mystics, the energy created by children playing on these branches takes on the enormity of a prayer whose power is at the same time life-giving and life-changing. Consider for a moment the magnitude of influence the cloistered monastics have on the world. What kind of experience would we have without them? Without their contribution of peace-offerings through prayer and loving intention, without their love and gifts, the world's hate, disconnection, and discord would surely overflow and offer little hope of forgiveness or harmony. In much the same way, children's spiritual life force touches the world.

These children demonstrate their spiritual gifts and awareness on one, several, or all of the branches depending on their spiritual intelligence; their gifts and characteristics are transformed into a living, animated world as complex as the ecosystem of a real tree. The interconnectedness of the seven branches creates a healing life force that dynamically encompasses the children, their families, their communities, and the world. Their now-interrelated gifts, characteristics, and experiences become powerful resources, carrying with them the potential for change, growth, and inner and outer peace from which all can benefit.

Encouraging Your Child's Spiritual Intelligence has seven chapters organized around each of the seven branches of the Spiritual Tree of Life. Each chapter ends with "What to Know, Say, and Do," a practical guide to help spiritual partners confirm, comfort, and communicate with their spiritually gifted children. The afterword, "Spiritual Partners in Today's World," addresses the critical need for spiritual partners to identify, nurture, support, and protect these boys and girls while they join their children on each branch. As spiritual partners are inspired by this mystical journey, their own prevailing forces, gifts, and capacities will come alive.

The seven branches of the Spiritual Tree of Life embody the gifts, rites of passage, and experiences associated with spiritual intelligence. The *first branch* depicts spiritual children's gifts of *wisdom and intuition*; the *second branch* represents their *profound compassion* coupled with their need for *belonging* and *connection*. The characteristics of these two branches are intertwined, making it nearly impossible to experience one without the other.

The *third branch* embodies spiritual children's belief that *death is permanent only in a physical sense*. On the *fourth branch*, they *participate in a world*, both invisible and incomprehensible to most adults, that primarily *consists of spirit*. Acting as spiritual warriors on the *fifth branch*, spiritual kids are sensitive to the notion of *light and darkness, good and evil*. On the *sixth branch*, they spend much of their time in a world of metaphor while engaging in *healing play*.

The *seventh branch* concerns the *transformative journey* many spiritual kids undergo as they shed their old lives on the road to spiritual rebirth.

Although all kids who demonstrate spiritual characteristics rest on at least one branch, occasionally there are children who, because of their nature or circumstances, involve themselves in healing play on each branch. Four-year-old Kyle is one of these children. The death of his older brother James in a car accident thrust him forward on an intense journey of personal and communal growth.

As he rested on the first branch of the Spiritual Tree of Life, Kyle repeatedly demonstrated his wisdom. For example, a few days after James died, a neighbor approached Kyle and his mother. Kyle's mother sadly told the neighbor, "Yes, we lost James." Kyle, who was three years old at the time, was listening closely and responded, "Yes, he was lost, but now he is found. God found him!" On another occasion Kyle knew I would be speaking at a conference about spiritual children. He told me to tell everyone, "People are really in good care, because they have angels and God."

On the second branch, Kyle established his compassionate connection with all people during a group meeting with children his age. After leading the children through a meditation and while their eyes were closed, I asked them who they saw standing in front of them. Kyle excitedly reported, "Mollie, I see all the people in all the world who have ever died—the Japanese are here too. And my brother is at the head of them all. I love people everywhere—all over the world."

Kyle also enjoyed playing on the third branch, where death is described as being permanent only in a physical sense. In the playroom Kyle was always accompanied by James. On several occasions he commented that James was not in the ground, "he's in heaven— and here!" Kyle spent much of his time playing on the fourth branch, which emphasizes that spiritual children live in a world that is not necessarily earthbound but that primarily consists of spirit. While Kyle played out his involvement in many invisible worlds and communicated with other unseen spirits, his interaction with angels was the most remarkable. Glowingly he said, "Mollie, your angels are always with you in the playroom! You have dozens of them." His hands reaching up over his head, he continued exuberantly, "There are lots of angels filling this whole room! Mom has lots of angels. My brother has lots, and dad has lots."

During several sessions he rested on the fifth branch, where he acted out the role of a spiritual warrior compelled to create a battle-field where darkness is transformed into light and good defeats evil. Six-year-old Kyle spontaneously created the following picture. At the bottom of the large easel in the playroom he first drew a circle with a plus sign ⊕ inside of it. Connected to this circle and trailing upwards is what he referred to as a path. He said, "The circle with the plus sign ⊕ inside is 'us' and we are OK, if we stay on the path where animals live, where there is a river, and lots of food, mostly in stores. We are safe there, until we get to the top of the path where there are more large circles, followed by similar circles surrounding the path." Pointing to the neighboring circles, Kyle said, "All of these circles are evil. It is all around us." He quickly added, "The food at the top of the path nearest the first circle of evil belongs to us, but it is being eaten by the evil ones."

Kyle spent most of every session on the sixth branch, in healing play. He created uplifting metaphorical stories symbolic of his journey.

Finally, resting with some apprehension on the transformative journey of the seventh branch, Kyle played out stories of his spiritual rebirth.

Play Therapy

Many of the children who are in play therapy with me have undergone severe losses or trauma, such as in the case of Kyle, whose older brother died in a car accident. Or they may feel oppressed by their uniqueness, as did Scott, whose concern and compassion was greater than the children around him understood. The stories in this book will show you some of the difficulties these kids have experienced. However, it is important to understand that boys and girls do not have to be traumatized in order to be spiritual children. In fact, many spiritual children are well-adjusted kids who may still struggle with a lack of support of their gifts.

A great number of boys and girls involved in play therapy merely need help making troublesome adjustments to difficult situations. These may include a move, the birth of a sibling, a change of schools, friends moving out of the area, siblings leaving for college, stepfamilies coming together for the first time, as well as divorce, even an accommodating one. Other populations of children that benefit from play therapy are ones who have developed a specific fear, such as that of animals, people in general, or even occasionally something as simple as potty training.

Sometimes the intellectually gifted enjoy the benefits of play therapy in order to become well-adjusted individuals with a special set of needs. Many others are struggling with poor self-esteem as a result of unsuccessful academic or social endeavors. Any or all of these children may be spiritual girls and boys who suffer additionally as a result of not understanding their giftedness. Their self-concept easily becomes that of a misfit in a world that cannot see or appreciate them for who they truly are.

The beauty of play therapy is that children do not need to rely on words to express their feelings and experiences. Play is their language—their way of living, emotionally and spiritually, while communicating this life to others. For example, most children whose parents are divorcing will spend a great deal of time in the sand table enacting a war between two sides; a girl who was recently adopted played out the story of a family with a new baby in the dollhouse.

In therapeutic play, which preferably, although not necessarily, takes place in the presence of a therapist, boys and girls first create and then transform their worlds of discomfort, and even trauma, to a world of hope, happiness, inner peace, freedom, belonging, and growth. Whatever they imagine in their play is as real to them as those destructive happenings elsewhere over which they had no control. In this nurturing milieu they are able to tell and transform their stories. For instance, if Susie's dog is missing, she plays out this sad story and then adds some healing element such as a nice family finds and cares for the lost dog.

My therapeutic playroom is brimming with imaginative ways in which children can express who they are, where they have been, and where they are going, as they communicate their struggles, feelings, triumphs, and joys. While my playroom includes such creative toys as an easel, sand table, kitchen area, playhouse with furniture and figurines, dinosaurs, farm animals, Lego building bricks, dolls, bottles, and clothing, as well as Play-Doh and art supplies for any number of projects, I have a preponderance of both arm and hand puppets.

One of the most popular of these is a large, brown, very fuzzy, furry, and lovable arm puppet named Freddie. Freddie has one very entertaining although sometimes irritating habit: he eats boys' and girls' shoes. When children hear about this, they usually smile and either hide their shoes or humorously offer them to him. Freddie is one of several playroom mascots that serve to put kids at ease. Many children have preferred to share their stories, or even their secrets, with these puppets before telling me or anyone else.

Play and imagination are a child's way of remaining balanced and healthy while moving out of a state of conflict, maturing, and developing more positive attitudes. Play therapy creates these beneficial results by providing a basic environment of freedom of expression, recognition, and acceptance. My role as a play therapist is to help the child client to be as comfortable as possible, at once feeling safe and acknowledged. Following the invitation of the child, I gradually become a trusted helper, whose goal is to enhance the emotional and spiritual well-being of boys and girls alike. I work together closely with parents, sometimes inviting one or two members or the whole family into the playroom for a session with their child. When needed, I teach parents how to be helpful between sessions.

Parents from other geographical areas often ask me how they will know which therapist, or anyone working closely with children, to choose for their spiritual child. I suggest that they refer to the self-quiz at the end of this introduction for appropriate inquiries. They may even ask a prospective therapist to respond specifically to the actual questionnaire. Perhaps they would be willing to read this book or others listed in the resource section. It is crucial that a therapist understand, or at least be open to, spiritual matters so that our children will not suffer with diagnoses of pathology when they are in fact dealing with the intricacies of giftedness.

It is important that all who work with children are open, objective, attentive, well-grounded, kind, gentle, unconditionally accepting, compassionate, playful, wise, and emotionally stable individuals who understand children and their parents from the perspective of their spiritual worlds. In relation to therapy with boys and girls, the importance of a playroom and a therapist who appreciates the value of play and is trained to engage with children in play therapy must not be underestimated. You can locate a play therapist in any state by contacting the Association for Play Therapy (APT) at the website in the resource section of this book. At the same time, individual referrals from spiritually-minded adults are invaluable.

Sacred Vessels of Our World

Our world is blessed with spiritual children who give to us an abundance of heart, incredible gifts, and unconditional, compassionate caring. These children grace every country, culture, color, and creed. They are the strength and hope not only of all our tomorrows but of all our present days as well—reminders that we, too, are rich spiritual beings with great purpose and value.

I promise you that spiritual kids will teach us, their adult partners, lessons we must learn, inviting us to be a part of their invisible worlds and imparting to us many wonderfully healing messages. Hungering for our acceptance and support on their spiritual journeys, their strongest desire is that we embrace them unconditionally as the valuable spiritual beings they are. Precious gems in our world, they transform our lives with their magical stories of hope while they teach us important lessons from their wisdom, innocence, and creativity. Their torches are forever burning even in the face of evil and destruction as they unite our global family in hope, freedom, and peace.

Please note that the narratives in this book are based on true stories. However, the children's names have been changed and their identities protected. I have sometimes combined a couple of related stories into one, since many spiritual children express themselves in a similar fashion. For the most part, the stories are told precisely as they happened.

In all cases involving spiritually gifted children, when you have concerns about your child, consult with a professional who is spiritually aware.

Self-Quiz
Are You Spiritually Gifted?

This questionnaire is for adults to answer, both for your child and for yourself.

This is a preliminary assessment of your or your child's spiritual intelligence. It will give you an idea of which of the seven branches of the Spiritual Tree of Life you each inhabit, and to what degree. It is merely a gauge or a reference point so that you can conceptualize how you both interface with this book—a moment in time that marks a place from which you can continue to evolve as well as to reclaim your spiritual child within.

Answering these questions is not a black-and-white process. By no means are the results frozen in concrete. Your individual scores are nothing more than a guideline that may lead you to discovering other branches on which you may enjoy resting. Perhaps not all the questions are relevant to you, and more questions may need to be added. Remember, we are pioneers in this fascinating world of the spiritual child.

I am a clinician who has discovered the spirit world in children's lives. While this questionnaire is hopefully an aid on your journey, I am more than aware of the possible conflict in trying to quantify spirituality. In regard to the mind's capacity, it *may* be appropriate to refer to it as having a greater or lesser degree of intelligence. But the spirit, in and of itself, has insurmountable potential that may not be evident from a questionnaire. In other words, there is no real possibility of a finite score. The Spiritual Tree of Life is ripe for expansion!

However, as you absorb the heartfelt stories of spiritual children and respond to the helpful suggestions within each chapter, your consciousness will expand. In a few weeks, take this questionnaire in hand for a second time. You will be amazed at the awareness and wisdom that has been rekindled in you and will be blossoming in your child.

Ask yourself the following questions and rate the intensity of your answers as *Often* (3 points), *Sometimes* (2 points), or *Never* (1 point). Which of these characteristics or experiences are about you or your child?

First Branch
Wisdom and Intuition

1. Do you feel that you have a special purpose or job to do on earth, such as that of a teacher, healer, peacemaker?

2. Do you sometimes intuitively sense that "all is not well" in your world?

3. Is living, knowing, and telling the truth important to you?

4. Do you think outside the ordinary?

5. Do you sometimes have dreams about things that happen later?

6. Do you ever just know without anyone telling you that something is going to happen and then it does?

7. Do you have an inner voice that acts as your guide helping you to make wise decisions?

Second Branch
Compassion, Belonging, Connection

1. Do you have an all-embracing concern for others?

2. Do you thrive on connection and belonging, realizing a meaningful relationship to all people despite nationality, color, or creed?

3. Are you profoundly affected by the plight of others, such as those afflicted by an earthquake, flood, or otherwise, near or distant?

4. Are you a sponge that unwittingly soaks up your family's, as well as others', distress with a burning desire to heal such suffering?

5. Do you feel it is key that we love and support one another as brothers and sisters?

6. Do you know kindness toward all persons and animals as you reach out to protect our country as well as our world, feed the hungry, clothe and house the homeless, defend the underdog, while safeguarding Mother Earth?

7. Do you treat others conscientiously with scrupulous honesty and fairness?

Third Branch
Physical Death

1. Do you have an ongoing relationship with someone who has died?

2. Is your grief journey enhanced by communicating with one who has died?

3. Has your mourning eventually given way to a realization of joy and completion, in part brought about by the involvement of the deceased person in the ongoing process?

4. Are you drawn to be engaged in a supportive fashion with those who are dying?

5. Once you receive comfort from a deceased loved one, are you more compelled to reach out lovingly to others?

6. While keeping the connection alive with deceased loved ones, do they talk to you, perhaps help you find things you lost, and stay with you much of the time?

7. Do you have a sense of belonging with those who are grieving?

Fourth Branch
A World of Spirit

1. Have you had encounters with imaginary friends or spiritual companions, such as angels, elves, fairies, or others?

2. Are your spiritual companions an important part of your life, worthy of recognition and celebration?

3. Have you had near-death experiences or memories of past lives?

4. Have you ever had dreams about flying?

5. Are you very creative with a vivid imagination?

6. Have you ever seen rainbows, lights, or colors around people?

7. Have you ever had conversations with God or another spiritual being?

Fifth Branch
Light and Darkness, Good and Evil

1. Is the struggle between good and evil very real to you?

2. Have you learned as a spiritual warrior that you have power over darkness or evil?

3. Do you identify perversion, destruction, and hate as evil forces you are compelled to defeat?

4. Do you recall battling evil (metaphorically or literally), perhaps as a spiritual warrior?

5. Does your battle against darkness take on the power of a prayer?

6. Have you felt, almost from birth, that you were determined to rid the world of evil while promoting peace?

7. At the same time are you aware of the presence of God or goodness?

Sixth Branch
Healing Play

1. In your play (in the past or now) have you been transported out of your everyday awareness?

2. Do you enjoy the benefits of imagination and creativity?

3. Have you found value in expressing your feelings and life experiences through verbalizations, play, art, and other forms?

4. Have you played out stories (in the past or now) about a variety of personal issues, such as your parents' divorce, the death of your dog, the hurt incurred by a bully, or other experiences?

5. Did the playing out of these stories help to transform your once troubled world?

6. Do you remember (in the past or now) feeling a sense of freedom, relief, or balance from your play?

7. Have you been instrumental in helping to bring to light traumas about which no one has spoken that may have occurred many generations earlier in your family?

Seventh Branch
Transformation

1. Have you journeyed through the "long, dark night of the soul" during times of great loss and turmoil?

2. Did you find yourself weakened to the point of almost not having a will to live when riding these rough waters of transformation?

3. Did you feel that you were stripped of everything that once served to keep you secure?

4. Did you experience such great transformation that it was like "death" as a shedding of your old life on the road to spiritual renewal?

5. Was your capacity to connect intimately with others and believe in the goodness of the world deepened?

6. Were you challenged to revisit parts of yourself and redefine who you are in the light of your altered world?

7. During this painful transformation, was your relationship with God or your higher self intensified?

The higher your score for a particular branch of the Spiritual Tree of Life, the greater your inclination to play on that specific branch. Your spiritual intelligence is clearly focused in this area. Since 21 is the highest possible score on each branch, 16–21 points would indicate that you are resting solidly on that specific branch. A score of 8–15 points is an average rating, where many people explore possibilities without fully claiming the gift. Anything below

7 suggests that this is a branch of which you possibly have little firsthand knowledge.

As an adult, it's likely that while considering these questions, a memory of your own spiritual child within has been awakened. As you go through this book, you can see how, given encouragement in the form of validation, nurturance, and support, you may be on the verge of rediscovering those precious aspects of yourself lost in childhood.

Your child's score is simply a guideline to help you. Remember, almost all children have some degree of spiritual intelligence. However, if your child's score is average or above on one or more of these branches and if your child seems to be having health, emotional, or behavioral problems, he or she may be dealing with inner or social issues related to misunderstood spiritual gifts. With the guidelines suggested in this book, it's my hope that you, as this child's spiritual partner, may gain the knowledge and understanding to enhance these gifts and support your child's joyful development.

Wisdom
and Intuition

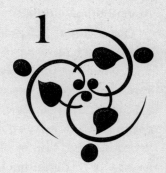

When I mention the words *your spirit* to kids on the first branch of the Spiritual Tree of Life, they rarely ask, "What's that?" They do not question whether their spirits are real. Try it! You may be delighted with their answers. They instinctively know I am talking about their precious inner lives where the wisdom and insights lie that are so enriching to them.

While becoming better acquainted with children on the first branch, I realized that they share closeness with truth that older individuals usually have lost. This wisdom is at their core of spirituality; they are indisputable healers while blessed with profound insights, intuition, understanding, and vision that come effortlessly to them. These insights and knowledge, whether from dreams or when awake, take them beyond their ages and immediate experiences and allow them to see outside the ordinary. Privy to information never directly or consciously communicated to them, they sometimes predict events while enjoying knowledge of their past lives.

Benjamin Hoff in *The Te of Piglet* describes wisdom as the natural state of a child:

Children are born with it; most adults have lost it, or a good
deal of it. And those who haven't are, in one way or another,
like children. Is it a mere coincidence that the Chinese suffix
tse, which has come to mean "master," literally means "child"?[2]

I remember the Native American women who shared their children's stories when I presented a workshop on children's spirituality in Sedona, Arizona. One told me of her four-year-old grandson who repeatedly said he was going to die. He asked if he could bring his little brother with him when he went to heaven. I was very touched by the grief of this grandmother, who remembered telling her grandson, "No, you are not dying! Both you and your brother will be here for a long time." Within six months the boy developed headaches and died of a brain tumor.

The grief-stricken grandmother deeply regretted she had not validated his awareness in order to help him draw closer to his family during his last months—to grieve and to say his good-byes. His inner wisdom was met with fear rather than with acceptance and encouragement. Fear prevented him and his family from preparing in a deeper, more spiritual fashion for his death.

Lisa

Occasionally, a child on the first branch will remember a past life, perhaps even minute details of it. For most spiritual children, this is an unnerving experience for which they get little or no support. As four-year-old Lisa timidly described the following events, she seemed to feel a great deal of guilt and insecurity. At the same time it was clear she believed in her story.

I used to be an African queen. I remembered that when I was
very little. I wasn't even two years old. I lived in a strange
land. Most people were poor and black. I was black, too. But I
wasn't poor. I was very rich and powerful. I told everyone
what to do. I tried to help the poor people get food for their chil-
dren. I remember this very clearly. I told my mother and she
did not believe me. She said I must have seen that on a movie

or something—that I was making it up. She thinks I'm lying,
but Mollie, I know it is true. Please believe me!

Dylan

Dylan, another astonishing kid who plays on the first branch, is blessed with insights into his hidden ancestry. Even though his adoptive parents had never told him about his heritage, in his play he described with astonishing accuracy the splendid Native American culture to which his ancestors belonged.

Although at birth Dylan weighed more than six pounds, a few days later he lost more than a pound and was not prospering. His original adoptive parents backed out at the last minute, leaving his life on hold. Although he was provided for during his first two weeks of life, he was without a loving person truly invested in his welfare.

However, by the time I met him, his energy and excitement were contagious, filling the room with expectation of greater things to come. Everything about him was big, including his thoughts about life, his ideas for imaginative play, his voice that boomed with excitement, his black eyes that danced with anticipation and were two shades darker than his skin, and his tears and fears when he talked about his mother's diabetes. As I became better acquainted with him, I realized that he was also undoubtedly a giant in his capacity to be a spiritual child on the first branch.

Dylan believed that each of us has a unique power.

My power is that I can turn into something and shoot fireballs.
Then I change into one-half butterfly, one-half praying mantis,
one-half bird, one-half octopus, and one-half hamster. Mollie,
you don't see me, because I am invisible. What is your power,
Mollie? I get little and big pulling a bag full of puppets. I am
invisible, but you can hear me. Just pretend the bag is moving
and opening up by itself.

As Dylan turned five and then six years old, his spirit was abounding with healing rituals akin to those of his ancestors of the great North American tribes. For instance, without any outside influence he was drawn to stones, believing in their mystical powers to help people on their journeys. He proudly shared the Apache teardrop, symbolic of the sadness in his life he brought to most of our sessions.

In one of his playful dramas, there was a house full of witches, vampires, robots, baby dinosaurs, dragons, and a wolf. Dylan exclaimed in a somber tone, "The wolf ate Freddie's (the furry arm puppet's) essence. Then his essence flew back into him when the wolf died." Six-year-old Dylan was using *essence* to refer to the spirit of a creature as though it were a natural part of a first-grader's vocabulary.

Then Dylan turned to me, saying in all seriousness,

You and Freddie and I must dance now, so the birds can go free! I healed the birds and the butterflies just like a doctor does. I made the birds all better when the T Rex hurt them. They are alive. They must be free! We will dance and we will scream. Our screaming will have a special power to kill the bad guys. After we scream, we will sing and dance. Our singing will bring the bad guys back inside their bad houses, so then I can kill the evil spirits. Mollie, let's dance and scream!

So Dylan and I moved in a circle, dancing and screeching with indistinguishable words and sounds. Once again from his innate wisdom and without his conscious knowledge, Dylan's ceremonial play was reminiscent of celebrations from Native American spirituality.

Using dark earth colors such as brown, gold, black, and copper, during one of our last sessions Dylan drew a picture of a boy dancing feverishly, as though with ritualistic movement. He wore moccasins and a light brown tunic with matching brown pants. His skin was dark; he reminded me of a Native American boy. I asked Dylan if this were the case. He looked at me confused and said, "No, Mollie, he's just a boy!" Then he drew a cocoon between the boy's legs as he cried, "Look, a butterfly has been born! He is flying up to the sun!" Dylan was indeed giving birth to the totality of his spiritual self as he flew to the source of light and love. He enriched all aspects of his life by playing out many unconscious aspects of his ancestry. Prospering on his journey, he became intimate with a growing sense of freedom to enjoy his birthright as a spiritually gifted boy.

Peter and Monica

When spiritual children are living in the household, they will often unconsciously absorb their parent's pain, both physical and emotional. Although not aware of their mother's physical symptoms or of the words she chose to describe her discomfort, twelve-year-old Peter and eight-year-old Monica both reported symptoms similar to their mother's. They had never discussed those feelings with her or with each other.

One morning their mother told me, "I have tightness and pain in my shoulder and my chest. It is an area that I would imagine looks like black tar." Later that day Monica told me, "I have tightness and pain in my shoulder. I call it a black blob." An hour later, Peter talked about having similar tightness in his chest. However, he described the same stiffness as a "red triangle, more like a pyramid."

Jonathan

As I ponder the wisdom and intuitive nature of spiritual children, nine-year-old Jonathan comes to mind. He was a remarkable boy with an extraordinary gift for predicting events even while brokenhearted over many losses, especially the recent death of his grandfather. Additionally, when he was about two years old, his baby sister died just two days after her birth. Jonathan had not been sure he had wanted a baby in his house, intruding on his space and robbing him of the attention he so urgently needed. When she died, he blamed himself. Unbeknownst to his parents, Jonathan's babysitter was abusive to him, emotionally, physically, and sexually. She put Jonathan in a dark, partially finished basement in her home while the other children ate or took naps. He would normally cry himself to sleep and then wake up alone, cold and scared. A furnace in the basement made frightening, creepy noises. He believed it was a monster.

As Jonathan was struggling with these painful memories, his spiritual gifts, including intuitive knowledge, were blossoming. He referred to his inner voice, which helped him on his life's journey, as his inner core. Drawing a picture of it, he explained, "This picture is about a dream I had about my inner core. That inside part of me sometimes said, 'Jonathan, you have to be scared!' Then I would be very careful about what I was doing." On several occasions his inner voice helped him to make wise decisions and to avoid harm for himself and others.

One day Jonathan was at a nearby lake with a group of boys and girls from the YMCA. They had just arrived when he began to feel anxious. His inner voice told him there was someone nearby experiencing a great deal of emotional distress and that he and his friends should wait to go into the lake. Cautioned by his intuition, he climbed an embankment with some friends and saw a man swimming to the middle of the lake, past the lifeguard and restricted swimming area. Again Jonathan's inner voice told him the man was intentionally endangering his own safety.

He and his friends watched as the swimmer began to sink under the water. Jonathan and his friends decided to see if they could be helpful. By the time they got to the other side of the lake, the man's still body lay on the beach. Although the newspaper article described the man's death as an accident, Jonathan was convinced he had committed suicide. He was saddened that, despite the information from his inner voice, he was unable to help the swimmer.

Presently, Jonathan is a very industrious young man with a gentle and awakened heart who has learned to appreciate the power of his intuition both in relationships and in his occupation. He continues to be given valuable information from his inner voice. His life is deepened and protected by this gift from which also flows a capacity for profound connection with others. His innate wisdom enhances his ability to give and receive love and to eventually let go of trauma that could otherwise be crippling.

As a result of the recurring pain of these children, they live an enriched spiritual life of great meaning, peace, and joy, using their gifts as resources that help them, and others, to survive and flourish. These spiritual gifts often include prophetic and intuitive knowledge of people and events that are communicated to them from an inner voice. This knowledge may create in them a considerable amount of distress, such as when they are not able to use the information they are given to help someone or even to save a person's life. As they enjoy the guidance of spiritual partnership they can learn how to utilize their gifts in such a way that they are not disturbed by their inability to always be helpful. At the same time their lives and our world will be decidedly blessed by their awakened presence.

Rose

Meeting Rose was a definite highlight of my last ten years. Never had I encountered a child with a name that so closely described her physical appearance as well as her spirit. She was a lovely, delicate, blonde four-year-old with rosy cheeks and skin that looked like a porcelain fairy. However, her beauty was not only skin-deep. Although she spent a great deal of time on several branches, her wisdom shone forth on the first branch, especially in her understanding of life and death.

From the beginning, Rose had been faced with an uncertain survival. Two weeks overdue, she went into fetal distress and was born with a dislocated hip following C-section delivery. For three months she was in a brace. Her hip healed amazingly well; by the time she was a year old, her physicians said she was perfect.

However, her physical problems continued: chronic ear infections despite the insertion of tubes, and urinary-tract infections that persisted to the time I met her, when she was four. Her mother said, "Rose is very emotional—she has stomachaches, she is preoccupied with death, jealous of her baby sister, clingy and insecure with me, and unwilling to sleep through the night if I am not with her."

When Rose entered my life, she was burdened with many sorrows, including the recent suicide of her uncle and the deaths of both maternal grandparents. She was still sad about the death of her paternal grandfather. Moreover, recently her mother had given birth to a baby sister, who served as another loss by robbing Rose of the center of attention.

As her eyes first met mine, I saw in them disbelief and skepticism born of her many losses. Yet her voice was gentle and trusting as she wisely remained loving and giving to others. Although physically small, her shoulders seemed capable of carrying more than many adults could manage. Her walk indicated stiffness not often seen in a young child. It was obvious that her sorrow was oppressive, adding stress to her days. Her quick glances in my direction suggested that she felt betrayed by life, perhaps by someone close to her. Before saying a word, her demeanor pleaded for help out of her grief and confusion. Her first question came from a deep, searching, and wise place in her heart: "Why can't you come back from heaven when you die?"

Rose did not hesitate to come into the playroom. She was instantly comfortable, exploring all the shelves of toys, especially in the kitchen area. Suddenly, she told me about an uncle who died a few months earlier. With tension in her voice she nearly whispered, "Nathan and Corey are my cousins. They live a few blocks away with their mommy. Their daddy died last summer. I get to see their father all the time. He visits me from heaven." Then, as she touched the playroom dinosaurs as though they were long-lost friends, she added thoughtfully, "I miss the dinosaurs. They all died! They were so cool!" She looked away as her face fell and her voice weakened. She spoke so softly that I had difficulty hearing her. "I'm not going to die until I'm sixteen. That's a long time away. Now I am young, but then I will be old!"

Rose seemed to be preoccupied with death. Speaking in a serious tone, she said,

Today we will play the Family Game. I will be the four-year-old. My uncle died and went to heaven. You can talk to my uncle in heaven without using a phone. Look, Mollie, he is buried in some of the sand. These are his bones. Before this, Tyrannosaurus Rex ate my uncle and swallowed him. Then

my uncle came back and visited me. After a while he said he was going back to heaven.

Then for several sessions Rose drew pictures of heaven. She said, "Mollie, heaven is watching over everyone! Sometimes heaven makes a storm and people die. Then heaven brings them up to heaven." She said we could visit her uncles in heaven, but we needed to be quiet in order not to disturb anyone. "Uncle Ben talks to me in the spirit of my heart, not in the sky. My heart knows what he says, but I don't." Rose was incredibly wise for her age, aware that she received the most important information in the spirit of her heart.

During the next few weeks, Rose's Aunt Marie died. Rose had spent many hours talking with her before her death. She even spoke to a church full of friends and relatives about the special times she had shared with her aunt, telling me, "I wasn't even scared." Rose no longer feared death.

Soon after Aunt Marie's death, Rose told me that her dog Jasper had cancer in his throat. She was hoping he would live at least eight more days, through one more Christmas. It was then December 16, and Rose was counting the days. She drew two hearts, expressing her concern and affection for Jasper. "The purple heart is for love. The red one is for hopeness." She paused and then asked warmly, "Mollie, can I visit you when I grow up?" Jasper survived a few more weeks, outliving Rose's wish.

Rose was anxious to tell me about Streaker, her new kitty. "I believe that my cat Fluffball who died is alive in my new kitten, Streaker. I believe every time a cat dies, a new kitten is born. I also believe that this is true for all living things. When anything dies, a new one is born." In her wisdom, Rose was aware of the gentle, but constant, transition from death to rebirth. Her experiences had taken her repeatedly to a place that she could not see with physical eyes. So much of her experience was otherworldly, dealing with encounters she understood in her heart and soul.

As the years passed, Rose has met many more challenges through the deaths of loved ones. She has learned to rely almost entirely on her spiritual resources, her profound insights, and wisdom beyond her years. Rose is ten years old now and has recently reentered my life to deal with her parents' divorce. Undergoing the distress of major changes in her life, she has been chosen as the president of her class. While still small of frame and very feminine in her approach, as a natural leader she speaks out dynamically on many occasions on issues impacting her school, church, and community. She is an honor-roll student who embraces her otherworldly nature and welcomes her experiences as gifts for a deeply enriched spiritual life rather than as liabilities. At times Rose's joy knows no bounds.

Lisa, Dylan, Peter and Monica, Jonathan, and Rose and are some incredibly spiritual children who have enriched my life with their gifts of wisdom, knowledge, intuition, and insights on the first branch of the Spiritual Tree of Life.

What to Know, Say, and Do
for Spiritual Partners on the First Branch

Children who rest on the first branch need a great deal of support from a spiritual partner, especially for confirmation, comfort, and communication. For example, if your child is healing to others or expresses the intention to heal, you might say, "You have a wonderful gift of healing. The world is lucky to have you—and so am I!" When appropriate, you may continue talking about being a healer, asking questions like, "What persons or animals would you like to heal now? Let's play that you are the healer and I am your helper."

Discuss the Spiritual Tree of Life and the possible involvement on each branch. Encourage your child with statements such as, "You are a spiritual child! When you were born, you came with lots of wonderful gifts and a kind heart!" Let your children know that their gifts are a natural and good part of who they are—to be enjoyed. Ask questions about the spiritual areas in which your child has shown interest.

Wise and intuitive children tend to also be ultrasensitive and idealistic. Point out the value of these qualities, while promoting the belief that "being different is good." Freely express your appreciation of their ability to intuit the truth and predict events. When validated and comfortable in their own skins, they will no longer need to absorb the world's sometimes harsh judgment of them.

These children need to understand that they cannot shoulder the pain of the world as much as they are motivated to do so. Taking responsibility for others to an extreme will only burden these individuals, perhaps creating a great deal of anxiety. Spiritual gifts are tools for enrichment, not to be confused with weighty obligations that lead to a great deal of turmoil. When your children are respected, believed, and supported by you as their spiritual partner, they can learn to be discriminating, sensitive, and courageous in the face of such demands. As they mature, they can freely choose, situation by situation, when to help others by using their intuitive knowledge and when not to become involved.

On the other hand, spiritual boys and girls need to be made aware that the very presence of their gifts demands that they follow ethical standards in their use. In other words, their gifts are tools for enrichment, not to be used to harm others.

Encourage your children to journal those things about which they feel responsibility, guilt, or shame, while keeping the door open for them to discuss with you these feelings. They must learn how to survive both the blessing and the frustration of being so sensitively responsive to a world that is at the same time welcoming and cruel. As you tell your own stories of being involved in situations in which you felt guilt and overwhelming responsibility, an enduring bond of support will develop between you.

Also keep a journal of the precious times your spiritual kids have taken the words right out of your mouth. Someday you will enjoy recalling those cherished moments with them. Expand the memoir to include the times they were intuitive about other people, such as predicting events and being aware of others' thoughts. A record of their dreams is also a valuable resource. Your journals and scrapbooks will encourage them to view their abilities as wonderful God-given gifts to be valued, celebrated, and used throughout life.

Open communication can serve to anchor your child. Without this exchange of ideas, spiritual children may experience a great deal of anxiety about heaven, death, rebirth, spiritual companions, eternity, and so on. As a spiritual partner, you are the anchor, and anchoring is vital for spiritual children to remain firmly planted in our reality while journeying to other worlds. By doing so, you create a resilient bridge between the worlds of reality and spirituality.

Appropriate touch will often decrease spiritual kids' tendency to carry stress. Occasionally, especially in extreme cases, professional massage is beneficial.

When you are aware of your children's need to play out an event, supplying appropriate toys to tell the story is as helpful as giving paper, markers, or pencils for creative expression. For instance, if a child is particularly drawn to dinosaurs, providing replicas or even handmade cardboard images will enhance the spontaneous expression of the journey. The metaphors you create can be greatly enhanced by using characters and events that arise naturally in the child's play.

Children on the first branch are wise beyond their years. As a result, they often intuit more than they can comfortably handle. If your child continues to show signs of distress for more than three or four weeks, consult with a spiritually aware therapist.

Confirm your kids' spiritual needs to express their wisdom, insights, and intuition:

- Respect, believe, and support their intuitive knowledge.
- Uphold the statement "Being different is good."

- Play out themes and metaphors about their spiritual lives.
- Keep a journal of their intuitions, both awake and asleep.

Comfort them:
- Accept and validate all their feelings, thoughts, and beliefs.
- Understand their poor self-esteem and guilt as well as their feeling of being overly responsible.
- Be aware of them as sponges for others' turmoil as well as the world's harsh judgment.
- Teach them not to shoulder the pain of the world.
- Spiritual gifts are tools for enrichment, not weighty obligations.

Communicate with them:
- Discuss ethics related to their gifts.
- Research their areas of spiritual interest.
- Encourage them to journal about their overly responsible feelings and guilt.
- Share supportive stories.
- Mutually explore your children's and your own spiritual lives while embracing each other's realities.
- Spiritual gifts are best recognized and enjoyed.

Compassion, Belonging, and Connection

Although spiritual children captured my attention with their vast reservoir of gifts and experiences, it took me much longer to realize that, just as important as their mystical experiences, they have several characteristics in common. These are the qualities of compassion, belonging, and connection—the essence of the second branch of the Spiritual Tree of Life.

Spiritual kids on this branch have an all-embracing concern for others while they reach out to the world with a love that has no bounds. They thrive on connection and belonging, holding most others in esteem as brothers and sisters, despite differences in color, creed, religion, and so on. In many respects the second branch is a difficult one because these children are often unable to screen out others' pain and have a burning desire to heal such suffering. They will never rest; they may become distressed, physically ill, or even suicidal if their goal of bringing about inner and outer peace is not reached.

Some of these spiritual boys and girls speak out for children across the globe who are afflicted with handicaps. Their message is, "The most important thing is that we love one another!" In some instances, adults who suffered losses as children reach out to help those who are grieving. These individuals may never travel far, but the impact they have on relieving suffering and bringing about peace is far-reaching. They know there is a universal thread that connects all of us; our appearance of diversity quickly melts away as we join together in the hymn of the universe.

Scott

Ten-year-old Scott was one of the compassionate kids. He played primarily on the second branch and suffered deeply from this vulnerable place. He believed that spiritually we are all related as one. Oneness was so natural and essential that he believed he could not develop spiritually or emotionally if his life were not focused on attaining at least a portion of this union.

Unfortunately, Scott was ostracized by most of his peers. This distressing feeling of alienation was tantamount to death, both physical and spiritual. The isolation led to agonizing feelings of self-doubt and even self-loathing. He was a spiritual child on a meaningful journey, torn between being himself and his desire for closeness with other girls and boys. In his confusion he felt like a failure, and sometimes life did not seem worth living.

He said with longing,

I want to make the world a better place, but it seems that a lot of kids like to start fights. It is very difficult for me when I play sports and no one chooses me for their team. I am standing there—the last kid while the others make remarks about me. I am closed out of the core group of boys who are jocks at my school. . . . I know that being different is OK, but it doesn't feel good to almost never be liked. Sometimes I want to die. I know that is not right—but when I am rejected so often, it really hurts. . . . I'm afraid for them to know who I really am, or I would be treated even worse.

Even with such oppression, Scott modeled the importance of kindness, valuing the uniqueness of each person and supporting the need for all children to freely express themselves without criticism. Scott's entire focus was to teach others the importance of love. Despite his age, he was compelled to heal the wounds of the world as though he were on a mission. Scott dreamed of being an author and as such would fulfill his desire to help the world become a better place while realizing the richness of his union with all those who would share his writings.

Everything he said, while usually spoken softly, convinced me he was a deep thinker: interesting, self-examining, articulate, and creative. He often talked passionately about the environmental and political needs of the world, realizing the importance of each person's awareness and action in response to those needs. He felt he had a responsibility to be the kind of citizen who protected our country as well as our world, who fed the hungry, and who clothed and housed the homeless. His unwavering wish was to safeguard Mother Earth, along with her occupants, from damage or ultimate destruction.

With great compassion, his father described Scott's feelings: "My son is an enormous threat in the classroom because he responds with great interest to the materials presented."

Scott told me sadly,

I think the boys are mean to me because I scare them. They probably would like to not always play sports. They don't really always want to be tough. They have good minds, and they would like to feel that it is OK to use them. . . . Maybe they are a little jealous of me. I just want to be accepted! It hurts me really bad when I'm not. I worry and wonder about what I will be like when I grow up. Will I always be rejected?

Meeting Scott a few days before Thanksgiving was more than appropriate; ever since I have been deeply grateful for the rare opportunity to know such an exceptionally spiritual boy who spends so much of his life on the second branch. By the end of junior high school Scott realized that his self-esteem was not dependent on the opinions of his peers. He connected with several other students who shared his fervor for learning and who greatly valued preserving

Mother Earth. He successfully put his energy into community projects. Despite the fact that he knew he was different because his paradigms were shaped by his spiritual talents and aspirations, he ultimately enjoyed a sense of belonging. An inspiration to others, he lives in a rich milieu of interconnectedness with a great sense of hope.

Rebecca

Rebecca's deep sense of belonging led her to an ever greater yearning for harmony in her relationships with family and friends as well as with the world. At seven years old, she was as strong spiritually as her appearance was physically delicate. Her eyes were soft and direct in their gentle communication of honesty and hurt. There were moments when she avoided eye contact; at other times she appeared to hunger for my eyes to connect with hers. Her hesitant speech told me she was not sure she could trust me.

When I first met Rebecca she exclaimed, "I do not like my brother! I wish that I were a boy! My whole family likes boys the best." She was jealous of the attention he constantly received. He made good grades and everyone liked him. Despite her nagging feeling that she was not as important because she was "just a girl," Rebecca still was a loving child who felt a deep affection for people and animals. Her caring for others made her incredibly vulnerable; she would become distressed when faced with the loss of a family member or friend or a natural disaster that killed hundreds of people in a distant country. At the same time, she described her heaven on earth.

> *This family is buying a huge home so that everyone in the entire world will live together. We will put a gigantic sun over the entrance to the house. All the kids and big people and pets will be comfy. Nobody will get hurt! If they do, everyone will take care of them. My home will be a happy place—not ever a scary one! Mollie, I want all the kids to be together in one room. All the old people, even daddy, will be together in another room.*

In the dollhouse, she spent all her time helping everyone, not only family members, to be "safe and warm and happy."

A year after Rebecca's last session I received a letter from her mother.

> *Rebecca is doing great! Clear as a bell. She felt frustrated and sad today sharing that she wanted a friend who was a better "match" than her recent buddy. She feels alone sometimes, and different. I remember feeling that way, too! I guess we just continue to cycle through it.*

Two years later came another note:

> *Rebecca continues to grow and never ceases to surprise us. She's so much a "Child of God," really embracing the concept of God within. She has a keen sense of love and justice and supports kids who are victimized by teachers, other kids, and life.*

Rebecca's light was shining forth, giving warmth and protection to her family, friends, and all those who needed her bountiful compassion and creative energy.

The boys and girls on the second branch teach all of us who are willing to listen invaluable lessons in compassion and connection, helping us to believe in the importance and uniqueness of each and every being. As such, they know kindness toward all persons and animals and are overwhelmed by the misfortune of others. Those who know them are deeply touched by their sensitivity to the suffering of all living creatures. They are gentle reminders of hope for a new tomorrow.

Brooke

Brooke also played primarily on the second branch. Her story is both a heartbreaking and compassionate one of the love and devotion a sister has for her brother as well as for all children who are hurting. Despite her parents' recent separation and impending divorce, Brooke, a stunning girl of Armenian and Hispanic descent, continued to approach life with hope and enthusiasm.

Her sense of compassion was incredible for a child her age. She treated others conscientiously with scrupulous honesty and fairness. Even in junior high school, Brooke never failed to defend the underdog and wouldn't contribute to harmful gossip. As I became better acquainted with her, I realized her remarkable compassion for her family, especially her younger brother, Shane, who had spinal muscular atrophy, a terminal disease.

When Brooke was thirteen, she spoke to her class.

[Shane] is afflicted with a disease called SMA, or spinal muscular atrophy, a genetic disease that affects the motor nerves of a person's body. When nerve cells die, the muscle cells receive no information and are no longer able to thrive. Muscle cells begin to die, and as a result the body begins to weaken. This process continues until death occurs. SMA is a fatal disease with no treatment available and no cures in sight.

When my brother was about eighteen months old, he was diagnosed. At first, I didn't understand what the big deal was. Then after a while I realized that when you really love someone, you want them to be able to learn and do as much as possible. I slowly learned that Shane would probably never walk or be able to experience the joy of moving about freely, something you and I all take for granted. All the dreams I had of all the things I was going to do with him were changed and some were now even gone.

. . . He is a great person to be around. He is intelligent and has a great sense of humor. He has lots of friends and is making more and more every day. He loves to talk and he always has something wonderful to say about everything. Shane knows he is different than others, but he doesn't say much about it. . . .

Every person has a test in life. Everyone has to get through that test as best he or she can. . . . Of all the tests life has handed me, the hardest one is Shane. This test has not yet been graded. I am glad I have a brother, and he makes me feel good. I love him very much, and I am glad he is in my life.

In later years Brooke wrote,

Because he can't move himself, he depends on my mom. Every night she or I lie with him while he is in pain until he falls asleep. Then on an average, he'll wake up two or three times that night needing us to turn him. Once every two weeks my mom gets a break! . . .

I don't want to talk on the phone with my friends or do my homework. I just want to lie with him and just let him know that I love him more than words, or poems, or tears can express. After that night I realized that someday he won't be there for me to hold. He told me the other day through tears, as I hugged him, "Brooke, I want to walk and jump. How come I can't? How come I am like this?" What could I say? I didn't have the answer. Who does? No one knows the answer.

Why do children suffer? The best explanation I can come up with is that they teach us! They teach us that no matter how bad we think we have it, we need to still persevere and show God's love, because there is always somebody who has it worse, like Shane. If he can come through with shining colors, so can we. Someday we can ask God why, and then all this pain and hard work will make sense.

Brooke is presently a pre-med student who readily shows compassion to those near her. Her greatest gift to others is her heartfelt message to them—that she too has suffered as a result of her unconditional love of another; that she has not only survived such an intense journey, she has been spiritually strengthened by its rigors. Her capacity for giving and receiving love has been greatly augmented.

Nina

Children on the second branch inevitably teach all of us about the profound connection between love and spirituality. Twelve-year-old

Nina was one of these unforgettable kids who blessed the world with her spiritual gifts. She was a beautiful Jewish girl who spoke with a gentle intensity. Her recent near-death experience had left her with an even more compassionate heart, more fully aware of her connection to all peoples.

Nina was strengthened by her close call, but her experience greatly altered her. She often spoke of it with family and friends, although Nina's father, who survived the accident with minor injuries, did not want the matter discussed in his presence. Consequently, Nina was afraid to tell anyone about receiving God's grace, love, and inspiring message of hope. Hesitantly, she explained to me,

Ever since the day I was in the car accident with my dad, I know how imperative it is that we all love one another. God told me! When I died, I saw a bright light at the end of a tunnel. I thought there was an angel waiting for me. When I got to the light, there were several angels and lots of people. Then God appeared!

Sometimes my friends, and even my family, get mad at me for talking about this. They want me to shut up. My parents took me to another counselor before you. I think they were scared that I was crazy or something. When I told the counselor about seeing God, she did not smile, or act nice, or anything. She just told me it would be better if I stopped talking about God. She said that if I didn't, I would make everyone mad at me, and I would get in trouble. Now I feel very lonely and sad at school and sometimes even at home. I feel like I have done something bad.

I felt such joy after seeing God that all I wanted to do was tell everyone what he said about loving all people. Luckily, now my mother believes everything I say. She just wanted me to talk to you so maybe I would not feel so lonely. She knows I don't lie. She told me that I am a very wonderful girl to have talked with God. She said that I am his messenger. She made me feel really important.

I know that talking with God is the most important thing in the whole world! After some people got mad at me, I decided for a while that I would not ever share my story again. Then I changed by mind; I don't even care if I get into trouble. My relationship with God is more important! His message was not a secret. He wanted me to tell everyone!

Nina found her connection with me to be healing. She glanced longingly into my eyes, asking, "Nobody can take away my time with you?" Then she answered, "No, they can't. Seeing you makes my heart feel better."

During one session, Nina, more pensive than usual, continuously built one mountain after the other in the sand table; then she would angrily destroy each. As she shaped and shattered several mountains, she told me that she knew about the Holocaust.

It makes me very sad to think about all those people leaving their homes and being killed—even kids! I'm not just sad because I'm Jewish. I'm sad mostly because it's bad for people to hurt other people. There are no excuses! When I met God, he told me, "Love one another!"

In the dollhouse she created five families. Then she made another mountain and buried all the parents and their children in it. With one tear streaking down her cheek, she told me, "They were all buried alive! Now they are dying in the sand, but no one can kill their spirits! Mollie, sometimes I want to be dead so my spirit will be free. I want to go visit God again."

Unfortunately for everyone touched by this incredibly spiritual girl, Nina and her family moved away. On our last visit, she told of the sting of rejection she continued to feel when her story was not appreciated. Despite her distress over nonbelievers' responses to her, with her mother's and my support Nina was learning to love herself even more after her meeting with God.

More often than not, children on this branch feel the suffering of others deep within them. Their hearts are awakened to the pain of discrimination, poverty, and the injustices suffered when people are persecuted because of differences in race, color, and creed. They also feel the pangs of knowing that the world does not always mirror their need for intimacy, justice, and peace. They hunger for the support of a compassionate community.

D.J.

D.J. was only an infant when his mother left him for several years. Luckily, his grandmother reached out to him with the same love she had so devotedly offered her children. With deep gratitude he repeatedly drew rainbows for her; he was finding his pot of gold in the love she so freely gave to him. By the time D.J. was nine years old, he knew his grandmother in only one capacity: as a mother who, most importantly, was his spiritual partner.

D.J.'s father felt only a minimal interest in his son. D.J. would sadly explain,

My father in Michigan did not come to see me after Christmas. I was so disappointed. I cried and beat on some pillows. I was so mad I said to Grandpa, "I hate you!" It wasn't true! I only wanted him to feel all the hurt I was feeling. So I said it! I really hurt his feelings, but he forgave me. He seemed to understand how bad it feels when my father does not keep his promises to visit me. I am black like him. That is very important to me.

My grandma calls me Chocolate Milk because my skin is kind of black and white. You see, my mother is white and my father is black. I wish I was really black like Martin Luther King. I mean really black! I've seen a lot of black people. I feel like I am part of them. They are the best at my sport—football.

When I met D.J., he was nine years old. His journey had already taken many turns, often involving death. Showing me his family album, he described several significant losses he had endured.

My two dogs, Red and Alf, died. Red died first. Alf had always lived with Red. He was heartbroken when she died. He could not live without her. He died within a few weeks. Then my uncle died. The same year my friend Nathan's father

*died in his sleep. Another friend had a daughter who was six-
teen. She ran away for two weeks. She didn't die, but we
were scared about what had happened to her. She finally
came home. Then Grandpa got hurt in a car wreck. I was in
two accidents with my mommy driving. A teenager tackled me
and made my eye bleed. My great-grandmother had to go to a
rest home. It seemed like we didn't love her anymore. She died
a little bit later. Now I think two more animals and one person
I love are going to die soon. My cat, Spook, is very old. Susie,
my third dog, will die someday, maybe soon.... Great-
grandpa is almost as old as Spook. So he'll probably die soon,
too. I am sad about my mom leaving. She worries me a lot.*

*I am so happy to be with my grandma and grandpa. At
my grandparents' house I can use a night light all I want. My
grandma also told me that I can cry anytime I want. So I do.
One time she forgot this rule. I was mad at her so I told her,
"Remember, you said I could cry anytime and anywhere I feel
like it!" Grandma said she was sorry and that I was right! She
makes me feel safe. I love her!*

His grandmother's compassion and empathy was very healing
for D.J., who found great personal freedom and responsibility when
he cried openly. He basked in the knowledge that he was loved and
accepted as himself. Because of her care he was able to give and receive
love, the deep-seated purpose of spiritual kids on the second branch.

"How much do you love me?" he had quietly asked his grandma
one day. As he told me the story, his demeanor suddenly changed to
an intense sadness and strength rolled into one. Staring at the floor,
he told me her answer: "I love you enough to let you stay with your
mommy all you want." He then turned to his grandma and said, "OK,
but do you love me enough to keep me?" His grandma gave him the
biggest hug ever as she said, "Forever!" D.J. paused, gazing into my
eyes, "She is my guardian angel on earth."

*I know my spirit is from heaven. It is the part of me that makes
me a better person. If I listen to my spirit, I do better things. Ever*

since my baptism, Jesus talks to me. He really is my best friend. He likes it that I love all the people of the world, not just the people who are like me. When I was really little, like three years old, I drew pictures about Jesus. I drew one about him when he died. I remember putting a cross on the front and inside the tomb. I drew him rising up to heaven. . . .

D.J.'s expression of his love for the world touched everyone who saw the paintings that so beautifully portrayed his spiritual journey, fulfilling his need to connect with his global family. Despite all his losses, he remained steadfast in his compassion for the people in his life. He became a leader in his school and was highly successful academically and in sports. As a spiritual teacher, he revealed to me the power of love that sustains each of us as we learn to accept the unpredictability of life.

All children on the second branch give to the world heartfelt messages of love. They are compelled by a profound need for connection and for the reassurance that all people have the chance to thrive. They are such compassionate and connected beings that if they are continually frustrated in their desire to enjoy a sense of belonging, it may become a matter of life or death for them. The world community is likely to benefit from their immensely caring hearts because they will not stop until they have righted wrongs and restored harmony and balance.

What to Know, Say, and Do
for Spiritual Partners on the Second Branch

Children who rest on the second branch need to know that when they are hurt by others, there is a safe place for them to retreat: to you, their spiritual partners. With this support they can gradually build a greater sense of self-esteem and a deeper, more aware acceptance of their irrefutable spiritual nature.

You can teach your children to set firm boundaries to protect themselves from the cruelty around them. Without this permission, encouragement, and knowledge, they may learn not to believe in themselves as their deeply spiritual nature is ultimately put at risk by a not-so-kind world. You need to make it very clear that you are encouraging them to pick and choose to whom they give the gift of compassion. They will learn to give only what they can comfortably offer. They must be encouraged to follow their intuition and to not relate closely to those whom they do not trust.

Sometimes kids on the second branch need your creative suggestions to enhance their sense of safety. For example, if your children believe in fairies, they may be taught the value of "fairy dust" you gather from your home, playroom, or classroom. Put this invisible, magical substance into an envelope marked with their name and *Fairy Dust*. They will be eager to believe that when they take the mystical powder home and place it on various spots in their room, it will continue to grow until it covers the entire house. Within the confines of the fairy dust, they will feel safe in a protective womb.

You can teach your children imagery that keeps them spiritually safe from the pain, invasion, and demands of others. For instance, with eyes closed they can envision a pulsating golden white protective light that they install throughout themselves; the light then continues to permeate and protect their family, home, neighborhood, and world. Directing spiritual children through this imagery can lead to incredible joy and relief for them.

Writing about their play world can benefit spiritual children in three ways: it provides them with a creative outlet, a way to bring about peace and healing in the world, and a means to more fully realize their closeness with those who share their writings. Tell these authors-in-the-making that their contribution to the world is extraordinary and that by journaling about their play, they may be preparing to be a philosopher, writer, or artist. Communicate these ideas with an attitude of support and freedom, not obligation and guilt.

Help your environmentally aware spiritual children to become involved in projects that protect Mother Earth. Realize that it is critical to their healthy adjustment to have at least one good friend who shares their interests and values. Expose them to a variety of kids so they can find a life-giving connection with another spiritual child.

Many spiritual children are sensitive to the pain in the world, which sometimes produces anxiety, stress, and guilt. Your child may show this tension by being irritable, hyperactive, or oppositional. You can sometimes alleviate these symptoms by letting your children express their sensitivity and concerns to you.

Discuss with spiritual children the basic characteristics of their spirituality, including their compassion and integrity, their honesty and courage. As a spiritual partner, point out how these characteristics relate to their friendships, the world, and, of course, themselves. Give them the clear message that you love, accept, and value them. It often helps these kids if you tell them relevant stories from your own spiritual journey.

A child's near-death experience and meeting God must be validated by the spiritual partner. A great deal of harm can be done to a child who is told that something as significant as this experience did not happen. Encourage your child to tell the story many times. Suggest journaling and illustrating the story. Expose your spiritual child to books and support groups regarding children's near-death experiences. Your child's incredible journey will enhance his or her joy for a lifetime and will motivate returning love to the world.

Children growing up with a chronically ill sibling are often overwhelmed by responsibility, guilt, and fear of losing the one they love. Spiritual partners are central to supporting these spiritual kids so they can preserve their gifts while having an outlet for their stress, anger, and resentment. They need to tell their story to someone who will listen with empathy—never disinterested or critical when they hear the same story many times.

Spiritual children are deeply connected to and trusting of those they love as well as people in general. Despite their strong sense of community, they may readily withdraw when injured by life's circumstances. Comparable in strength to their sense of oneness is their sense of betrayal if harmed or abused by someone they trust. Grief brought about by the death of a loved one can be overwhelming. Any major change in a spiritual child's already-compromised world will warrant additional support from spiritual partners such as therapists, doctors, nurses, church-related persons, teachers, and, of course, parents.

Help your spiritual boys and girls to celebrate life to its fullest and to find joy in sorrow, laughter from the simplest things, and blessings they count continually. This sense of celebration and gratitude will naturally fortify them against absorbing the pain of others. Meditation can also accomplish this goal.

Finally, as you direct your spiritual child, beware of judgments. "Lighten up!" or "Why are you so serious?" statements may strip spiritual children of their dignity and create the darkness and seriousness you are hoping to alleviate. With your growing knowledge, you will understand that they are not truly dark or unsuitably serious. They are merely using their gifts to navigate through a world that needs so much healing. Every day is a challenge for them to maintain balance and harmony in their spiritual world while being impacted by forces that could devastate them.

Children on the second branch are loving beings whose sense of oneness sometimes leads to a stronger sense of betrayal. As a result, they may withdraw due to their feelings of overwhelming guilt and responsibility. If retreating to you as a safe place for three to four weeks does not create a greater sense of self-esteem and acceptance of their spiritual nature, consult with a spiritually aware therapist.

Confirm your kids' spiritual needs to express compassion and to create a sense of belonging and connection:

- Enable your child to belong to organizations that may enhance belonging, such as your local church or groups that protect Mother Earth, fight hunger, or work for world peace.
- Realize the unquestionable connection between spirituality and love.
- Encourage friendships of understanding and appreciation with other spiritual kids.
- Promote the philosopher, writer, or artist in each child.

Comfort them:

- Appreciate your child's predisposition to anxiety.
- Offer them support groups.
- Teach them imagery to enhance their sense of protection, joy, celebration, and blessings.
- Anticipate severe reaction to rejection, especially by peers.
- Introduce them to fairy dust.
- Protect your younger children from exposure to disturbing news reports and other distressing programs.
- Help your older children to let go of world suffering.

Communicate with them:

- Continue to play out spiritual themes your child has demonstrated.
- Emphasize the importance of freedom of expression as an antidote to sorrow and loss.
- Be an empathetic listener.
- Identify and validate spiritual gifts of compassionate connection and belonging.

Physical Death

Children playing on the second branch of the Spiritual Tree of Life have taught the value of compassionate connection to their families, communities, and world. Now, as they play on the third branch, they challenge us to enrich our worlds by embracing a more fluid concept of death. According to them, death as we commonly know it does not exist. For example, Scilla insisted that we each select several dinosaurs. "The dinosaurs are in a war fighting to see who gets the dinosaur land. They hurt each other so badly that they can't move. Don't say *died*, Mollie. Just say they became weak and went away!" She refused to equate the passing of each dinosaur with the finality of the word *death*, equating it instead to its body becoming incapacitated and its soul moving on to another world.

With their otherworldly doors open, these boys and girls teach us to redefine death merely as a transition from a physically embodied life to one in the spirit with the possibility of ongoing connection to those still in the body. Spiritual children's mourning is a communal process in loving union with those who have died. Thus, their grief, although usually involving an immense amount of pain, can more easily give way to a realization of joy and completion. In this way grieving takes on new and hopeful dimensions because the person being mourned is part of the ongoing process.

Many spiritual children describe having frequent contact with deceased family members. They say that the loved one who has died not only visits but becomes their guardian or protector. I like to refer to these guardians as spiritual companions.

Devon

The inspiring stories of children on the third branch leads to our understanding of miracles. Devon has one of these stories. When I met him, he moved with a tentative, insecure, and distrustful air about him. He avoided my glance as though he were fearful I might not like him. He appeared to be very lonely and was not expecting much out of life. His father, fifty-five years old, was dying of lung cancer.

Devon confessed within our first few minutes together, "I used to get so mad at Dad, I wanted him to die. Now that he is sick, sometimes I want to die, too. Mom is always mad at me. She loves my little sister, and she thinks that I am a pain." He smiled as he spoke about feelings that tore at my heart. He appeared to have no expectation that I would care even a little. It struck me as tragic that a nine-year-old boy could feel so undeserving of love, caring, and attention. Despite his lack of trust, however, he spoke readily, with desperation in his tone.

> At first I thought that if my dad died, I would want another dad. Now I've decided that if he dies, he will watch over me. I won't need another dad. My mom and sister and I are going to be OK. Everyone is trying to make me feel good, and I like that. It's nice, because we have lots of help. I pray that God will make a miracle so my dad will not die.

Devon's prayer was not answered in the way he had hoped. Within a few days of our talk, his father died. When I saw him a week later, Devon appeared noticeably smaller. He held himself tightly as though he were afraid he might fall apart if he relaxed his grip on life. When he spoke, he choked back his tears.

I already miss my dad. I'm afraid something is going to hurt my mom, too. Then she will be gone, and no one will take care of my sister or me. It's really not fair that my dad died! Everyone in my family is mad and sad. I am trying to be perfect everywhere for everyone, but I'm never good enough! Everyone in my family is grouchy these days. These are bad days. I don't want to tell my mother how I feel, because it will make her sadder. She might even get mad at me. I know I am mad at her! I am even mad at myself for being mean to others, especially my sister. Mostly I'm mad at my dad for dying!

Devon spent a lot of time alone looking at his dad's picture, wondering how he was feeling, where he was spending his time, and what he was finding to do that interested him. At home and at school he was withdrawn, quietly moving into his own space without protest.

Sometimes I think it's my fault that my dad died. . . . I really want to hurt someone if they ever say something mean about my dad. I want to say, "How would you feel if something like this happened to you?" I want my rights. I don't want people to be teasing me. I heard some boys calling me bad names because my dad died.

One day Devon took a blue marker and quickly dotted my nose and then laughed loudly as he nervously drew a picture of his father. He threw Styrofoam balls at me while yelling at his father's picture.

Dad, I'm mad because you hurt my feelings. You make me sad! You make me very sad and mad! You make me cry! You make me feel really bad! I don't like it when you do that! I'm frustrated with you! My question is, "Why, why did you have to die?"

He took a gray marker and colored in the sky, writing over the picture, "I'm mad and sad! I'm mad and sad! Why did you have to die?" Then he sat down at the kids' table and looked straight into my eyes for the first time since his father died. I had become a haven—

a safe place where he could share his journey of grief without fear of criticism. He said as quietly as possible, almost as though confessing his sins,

> Mollie, remember when I asked God for a miracle? I asked him to not let my dad die? Well, he didn't keep my dad alive, but he did give me a miracle! He lets my dad talk to me sometimes when I am alone in my room. He also lets him be in my dreams. We are always doing fun things together. I had a dream a few nights ago. My dad talked to me in it. Then God gave me another miracle! When I woke up, I saw my dad in the room for a minute! He said to me, "I love you. I wish I didn't die." I felt really happy to talk to him. I didn't want him to go.

Although the miracle was not what Devon had requested, visiting with his dad was nonetheless a deeply spiritual life-changing experience. A few weeks later Devon told me another story of a miraculous visit with his father.

> I talked to my dad again last week! I told him that I loved him and I missed him. He told me that he loved me and missed me, too. It was awesome! I feel like he is here with me most of the time. He didn't really go away, Mollie! I'm still mad and sad sometimes, because it's not the same as before. But one thing I know for sure, my dad still loves and cares for me. And he will always be here with my mom and sister and me. I know he is watching over us!

When Devon visited with his father, he was not afraid because he felt that those contacts were gifts from God, miracles born of God's love for his family and him. When he realized that when his dad died he did not really go away, Devon's place of desperation became a spiritual monument of love and hope.

Sammy

Sammy was unusually sincere and forthright. At eight years old, his integrity, even in the face of tragedy, was one of his many striking characteristics. He was honest about his anger, his hurt, his love, his hopelessness, and his belief that because he had been abandoned once, he probably would be again.

Sammy spoke hesitantly, taking loud, shallow breaths. He held his body rigidly, as though not trusting that life would be kind to him. Although the words did not come easily, he was compelled to speak his truth: "Mollie, something good in my life is that there is a place where insects can hide. Two really bad things are that animals are killed and my dad killed himself just four weeks ago."

Sammy's mother described Sammy's father as a tormented man who had started drinking heavily over the past year after their separation and divorce. He began to lose interest in living, isolating himself with no significant social connections except for Sammy. Although already divorced, Sammy's mother deeply grieved the loss of her husband of nearly fifteen years and her son who not only loved and missed him terribly but secretly blamed himself for his father's death.

Sammy's mother portrayed Sammy as "a wonderful, active, bright, and very athletic boy, with a mind of his own, although reasonable and open to guidance from others." She said that he and his father rode a tandem bike downtown, and I remembered seeing them on their bike only a few weeks earlier. That day he had glanced knowingly into my eyes, as though desperate for someone, even a stranger, to penetrate the walls around his father. When we finally spoke of that meeting, Sammy instantly remembered me as well.

Sammy described his father as a very frightening person at times.

> *My dad was very strange. He scared me lots of ways, like by saying boo! and chasing me dressed in a leopard costume and roaring. It was not fun for me! Just very scary, like the way he died! Dad's body is at Colorado State University for research, but my dad is in heaven.*

Sammy's statement demonstrated that he understood death to be permanent only in a physical sense.

When Sammy played in the dollhouse, he would feel responsible for rescuing his parents. He said that he saved his whole family from burning with their house. Placing three dinosaurs under the sand, Sammy said,

These three dinosaurs under the sand are in heaven together. One dinosaur has great strength, like my dad before he got sick. He pushes away the sand like a wave. All the good guys disappear into a different dimension, a three-dimensional place. No one can see them! When they want to, they pop out. They are invisible—and they are really there at the same time. They are just like my dad, who is always there even though you can't see him. He is my guardian angel!

After Sammy realized the presence of his father as a guardian angel, he felt a deepening sense of peace. Everything became clearer for him. As a spiritual child on the third branch, he clearly demonstrated that in his sadness and joy he could be in touch with those people and animals whose souls had passed to another place, perhaps the heaven about which he spoke.

Taylor

When I met seven-year-old Taylor, her father's death was imminent. Taylor's family and friends sheltered her from the reality of his impending death. When he died, Taylor was devastated over the loss of the most important man in her life, a courageous soul who held on to her with love, compassion, and warmth.

The second time I met with Taylor, she told me sadly that her dad died soon after her mother and she had returned home after their first meeting with me. She was quiet, appearing to be resigned to her sadness and loss. Out of all the dozens of toys in the playroom, she insisted that the ghost figurine she designated as her dad be a visitor in the dollhouse, along with his family and friends.

Taylor was aware of each weekly anniversary of her father's death, saying, "Today it is eight weeks since my dad died." As her sadness prevailed, she told me tearfully,

Mollie, would you write this down? I miss my dad! I cry a lot when I think about him. I saw him and he looked like Casper. Even though he looked like a ghost, he did not scare me. I like it when I see my dad. I see him very often these days.

Taylor loved the constant visits from her dad. Although she missed the way it was before her father died, she delighted in spending time with him.

Mollie, my father protects me like he did when he lived with us. Now he lives somewhere else, but he still visits us all the time. When I see my dad now, sometimes he looks like a ghost, but most of the time he looks normal. When I see him, he moves around and around—kind of like flying. Dad came to kindergarten with me on my first day of school! He told me, "I love you."

Because Taylor was visited almost daily by a man no longer in touch with anyone else, she feared I might think she was crazy. But each time she told me about the visits, I accepted them unconditionally and gradually put her at ease as I told her about many children who were visited by deceased friends and relatives.

In a later session, Taylor was filled with joy as she began a letter to her dad. She asked me to speak for her father: "Dear Taylor, I love you more than life itself! I wish I could have stayed in my body so I could play with you. Even though I died, I am still your dad!"

Taylor responded eagerly, "Dear Dad, I can write the word *pizza*—Mom taught me. I can also say *archipelago*. I am much taller than when you were sick."

Dad's response through me mirrored the pleased father he had always been: "Dear Taylor, I am very proud of you—the things you know and the way you are getting so big! I watch over you every day! Love forever, Dad."

Sometimes Taylor would focus intensely, describing in her play events representing rebirth and transformation in her life.

A jet crashed down right on the spot where I buried a dinosaur. Then the jet took off again but crashed and was buried again! The humans and another dinosaur got buried. Then the jet came out alive, took off flying, and quickly crashed again into the dinosaur's mouth and into the mountain. . . . Then everything came back alive—the dinosaurs, the humans, the jet, and the lizard! First of all, they all died together. Now they can all live together! . . . They share the same earth—in peace!

To me, Taylor's message was clear, and I struggled to use words that were simple enough so we would understand each other. I told her that when there was death, destruction, pain, or loss, after an interval it was followed naturally by a time of magnificent transformation, like a phoenix rising from the ashes with newfound strength. For her, this transformation gave birth to a renewed spiritual life, a "rebirth" of her connection to those she loved who had died, along with a sense of belonging to others who were grieving.

Isabella

When Isabella was eight years old, her mother, thirty-three, was killed in a car accident. She had been a devoted mother who was so important to Isabella that her father described her as a life force for their daughter. In her anger, sadness, and grief, Isabella sometimes felt as if life were no longer worth living. She often cried out to her dad in desperation, "Life is not fair!" Her father understood the anguish behind this belief. He remained kind, patient, and deeply committed to Isabella, even when she directed her anger toward him with statements like, "You killed my mom, didn't you, Dad? Mommy went away, and you came back, and I never saw Mommy again. You killed her!"

When I met Isabella, about three years after her mother's death, her tears flowed freely.

Sometimes I just want to go away and be with my mom. I miss her so much! The day my mom died, Dad didn't come to school at all. When I saw him later, he said that she had died. I thought he was joking.

Even before her mother's death, Isabella was unusually comfortable with the notion of death. She had spent a considerable amount of time at a hospice where her mother had volunteered and had developed close relationships with several patients during their terminal illnesses. Her mother had helped her to accept that death was natural and not something to be avoided or feared. Therefore, I marveled at Isabella's lack of an ongoing spiritual connection with her mother. Most children I knew who had suffered the loss of a parent remained in communication with that parent for years, even into adulthood.

But Isabella did not believe she deserved the richness and comfort that contact with her mother might provide; she carried the burden of several secrets. After she began to trust me, she said,

Mollie, a long time ago after my mother died, I killed my hamster! I was feeling mad because the kids were teasing me. I didn't know how to be mad in a good way, so I took things out on my pets. I squeezed my hamster's neck too hard, and he died. I felt horrible, like a very bad person—so scared and alone! I never told anyone, but I think my dad suspects. Then when a boy at school told me, "You're bad and no one likes you!" I believed everything he said. That night I went home and pulled out all of my eyelashes—just to punish myself.

When Isabella acknowledged her "wrongdoing," she finally embarked on a journey of self-forgiveness and love, ultimately regaining openness to her spiritual gifts. She clearly recalled her mother's presence on several occasions, such as the night before she and her dad moved to be near her dad's job.

There were boxes all over the house. In the middle of the night I woke up and looked around my room. I usually don't get up at night. I don't know why I woke up that night. Maybe it was my dream, but it seemed like someone had called out my name. As I looked around the room, I saw a white light sitting on one of the boxes. I felt scared a little. I didn't know what it was. When I thought it over in my head, I realized that it was my mom!

Isabella appreciated a deep spiritual connection with God. She prayed that someone like her mother would always be there with her to help her with the challenges in her life. She seemed to get an almost immediate response.

A couple of nights ago I woke up, and there was a white light sitting in a chair in my bedroom. When I went to bed the chair was facing the other way. When I woke up during the night, it had been turned around and was facing me. In the morning the chair was still facing me. I knew that my mom had visited me again. I was not scared this time! I was happy she was there to take care of me! I know that my mother does not only visit once in a while, she is with me every minute of every day!

When Isabella was eventually able to allow her mother's reassuring presence to comfort her, she once again reached out lovingly to others. She became a rather remarkable leader in her class, challenging boys and girls alike to show compassion to people in need. She was extremely successful at her first season in soccer while playing on a team of unfamiliar girls from the other side of town. When they decided to have a party at the end of the season, Isabella and her father hosted all the team members at their home. She became close friends with many of these girls.

Mary

Before I met Mary, her mother said to me,

I am still losing weight after trying the last treatment the doctors suggested. I believe I am dying. My daughter is going to stay here with her father for three months, until the end of the school year, and maybe into the summer. I am too weak at this point to take care of her. It is important to me that she has someone special to talk to about all of this. My daughter really needs help. I don't think she can handle this alone—even with the support of her father, grandmother, and other relatives. I would like for her to know that we have met, so she will be more comfortable with you.

A year later Mary's mother died after a long battle with cancer. Mary withdrew from everyone, with the possible exception of her grandmother, as though fearful she would be harmed further if others knew how vulnerable she was. When I met her, she secretly checked out both the playroom and me. Then she said sadly,

Mollie, my mom died. I miss her very much. She talks to me. She helps me find things I have lost. She is with me all of the time. She is still inside of me. She loves me very much and is helping me to become happy with my life. My mother's father was Spanish. He died after my mother died. My mother's sister died before my mom. Several other people I love have died, too. Mollie, do you know any other kids whose parents died?

Like so many children on the third branch, Mary was still in close contact with her mother. Although she felt her presence every day, she missed her terribly and mentioned her often. She spoke of her with great affection, listing the things she missed the most. "My mother was always so nice to me, especially when I told her that someone or something had hurt me. She always made me feel better. I could talk to her. She held me and hugged me."

Mary was a very young yet accomplished artist like her mother. Expressing herself through her art helped her feel close to her mother. While especially feeling her mother's presence one day, Mary drew a picture about their ongoing connection. Mary thought of her own soul as the energy she had for loving and being loved; her "Soul Picture" was a globe surrounded by all the colors of the rainbow. Inside the globe was a beautiful tree with heart-shaped branches. The tree was next to a brook. The sun was shining and the sky was full of the rainbow colors that also encircled the globe. One red rose was lying at the base of the tree. Mary then drew a picture of two globes, one on top of the other, similar to the one she had just drawn.

Mollie, my soul is the globe on the top. My mother's soul is the one on the bottom. The waterfall that is flowing from my soul into my mother's is my love for her. I know that my love for my

mom will never die. She still loves me, too! That's why she watches over me!

Mary gave me the picture. Today it is still on exhibit in my waiting room as a reminder of a wonderfully spiritual child on the third branch. Mary's greatest teaching for the world is, "Love, the giving and the receiving of it, never dies."

On this branch, spiritual children refreshingly redefine *death* in a way that gives hope to those of us on a journey of grief. Repeatedly, these unbelievably spiritual boy and girls speak of their ongoing connection to someone they love who has died. With few exceptions, nearly all children I have met have shared that they have dynamic relationships with deceased loved ones, who often take on a protective and validating role, such as a guardian angel. As extraordinary as it may seem, the purpose of these helpful spirits is very similar to that of a spiritual partner.

What to Know, Say, and Do
for Spiritual Partners on the Third Branch

Be prepared to have open conversations with kids on the third branch of the Spiritual Tree of Life! Consider it an opportunity anytime your child wants to talk about death or its aftermath. When children announce heartbreaking news, respond, "I can see how much you are hurting. This is a very sad and confusing time for you." Watch for signs of hesitance to talk or a hunger to tell all. Follow their lead. Encourage, but don't push. Let them know that you are available to talk anytime, day or night.

Get ready to be vulnerable and honest, to be willing to journey back to sometimes forgotten and distressful places of grief. You must be able to speak freely about death. When children say, "My mom is dying," gently confirm their reality and comfort them in their loss. Such support is essential to their survival as spiritual people. Grieving will not "just go away." Never put a time limit on a spiritual or grief journey.

Enable your children while on the third branch to keep their connection alive with their deceased parent or anyone they love who has died, to enjoy their supportive and loving presence. They will usually describe meaningful encounters with the person who has died. Support communication with the deceased one through letters and drawings. Encourage them to create, play, and dialogue around the circumstances of death.

Children whose parents have died will often find that there is no safe place to speak of their grief with their peers, who, more often than not, refuse to validate their journey. Given this lack of support, these grieving spiritual kids are at risk for illness, depression, or insurmountable anxiety. They may need the additional support of a professional.

Talk to your spiritual children about the tendency of kids to be mean when they do not understand another's painful, or even scary, experience. Help them understand the insecurities of their peers so they will not give weight to the negative responses. Validate their feelings by saying, "These kids have really hurt your feelings! That makes me very sad. Most kids do not know what you know, but they can learn from you. You are their teacher!" In our Western society, spiritual children often do not feel OK about playing on the third branch. If they are not validated, it is easy for them to feel bad about who they are in light of their spiritual gifts. As they learn to shield themselves from the disapproval of others, they will be comforted by the belief that you respect their feelings.

Give them the opportunity to become part of a support group to help other grieving kids, as well as themselves, by sharing similar stories. Hearing that other kids have spiritual companions who are deceased helps your children to know they are not weird or alone. Be aware of community resources. For instance, hospice offers groups for children who are grieving.

Provide your spiritual children with toys that express who they are and what they feel, free time set aside for play, and your interest and involvement in the play. Introduce them to friends and activities that are fulfilling, such as scouts, church, or neighborhood functions.

Spiritual children in crisis have a tendency to be perfectionists and therefore feel they are not good enough. Their close relationship with spiritual partners tells them they are desirable human beings and reassures them they are appreciated for their insights into death as well as for their gift of connection with ones who have died.

Keep in mind the possibility that they may be blaming themselves for the death of the loved one. As natural as it is to keep their connection alive, I have found that sometimes children will not feel free to do this, especially if they are feeling guilty or responsible for the person's illness or "death." Remember that when guilt is present, it can be overwhelming and demoralizing, oftentimes leading to feelings of shame and of not deserving contact with the deceased one. Your spiritual child needs a safe place to express these concerns.

Spiritual partners must also be aware that children who have lost a parent fear they may lose the other parent, a scary proposition that would leave them destitute without support and love. Therefore, in the face of grief they find themselves feeling excessively vulnerable and insecure since they thrive on loving connection, especially with significant others. When they express this fear, you can validate and comfort them by emphasizing the unlikelihood of your imminent death and telling them that you have no intention of leaving.

Spend time expressing anger *with* them. This emotion is particularly uncomfortable for spiritual boys and girls because they flourish in the face of connection, not conflict. However, a large part of grief is an overwhelming feeling of anger that crests like a wave and subsides as quickly—for kids and adults alike. Soft nerf bats and balls are great interactive tools for dealing with these feelings.

When children report visiting with someone who has died, it may be cause for celebration: a cake with candles, a special dinner out, a new toy coupled with an embrace and the sharing of favorite stories about the celebrated one. Ask the children how they wish to celebrate.

Children on the third branch thrive on loving connection, especially with significant others. If they continue feeling excessively angry, shameful, vulnerable, and insecure for more than three or four weeks in the face of grief, keep in mind the possibility that they may be blaming themselves for the death of the loved one. If your encouragement as a parent or spiritual partner is not enough during these difficult times, consult with a therapist, who has the skills to connect with your child.

Confirm your kids' spiritual needs concerning physical death:
- Validate their belief that a loved one's death is imminent.
- Confirm their reality.
- Promote supportive community involvement, such as hospice.
- Encourage them to keep their connection alive.
- Celebrate a deceased person's birthday or visits.
- Affirm that a deceased loved one watches over them.

Comfort them:
- Provide good support persons who recognize and understand their spiritual nature.
- Reassure them that "life and love, although altered, still go on."
- Never put a time limit on grief; don't expect it to "just go away."
- Help them to understand the beauty of who they are in their grief and spirituality.
- Alleviate the belief that they are responsible for their loved one's death, which leads to guilt, shame, and self-blame.
- Be present with kids who are in contact with a deceased person, lessening feelings that they are alone and different.

- Let them know that the surviving parent has no intention of leaving, emphasizing the extreme unlikelihood of this event.

Communicate with them:
- Speak freely about death, including how their peers treat them.
- Provide freedom of expression about death through art, drama, play, and dialogue.
- Always listen with interest to their stories.
- Suggest to them that they express their grief by writing letters, drawing pictures, and making books and puppets about or for ones who have died.
- Express anger *with* them.

A World of Spirit

The boys and girls on the fourth branch of the Spiritual Tree of Life are not confined to the limitations of life as adults know it. Exploring their identities, these children live in a world that is both invisible and incomprehensible to most adults. They journey easily, both during sleep and awake, into domains in which they coexist and prosper.

Often, children seem to have a rapport with a variety of fascinating, even magnificent, beings such as angels, deceased relatives, and fairies, usually advocates who watch over and offer a sense of protection and safety in a not-so-friendly world. They develop a dynamic relationship with their helping spirits, whom they sometimes call guardian angels. I like to call them spiritual companions because of their predominantly friendly, even loving, dispositions.

Children who have spiritual companions report that they are greatly affected by them; these companions become as much a part of the children's world as their family members are. Most importantly, their role in comforting and ultimately healing all children, especially those who are grieving or traumatized, is paramount. They provide the necessary love and support so these distressed children can safely forge ahead with hope and courage.

Angels

Lana, a very intelligent eight-year-old, enjoyed the company of a guardian angel while she saw lights around people. When she was very young she often commented, "Mommy, the Christmas angel is here!" She communicated some of her special experiences through drawings, saying,

> This is a picture of the protective lights that are around me. I can see lights around you too, Mollie! Now, look, this is a picture of the energy that surrounds me. The force around me is strong, so I drew it in red. And this is my angel. She is a very good friend to me. She has energy around her, too. Sometimes at school I feel like I am getting sick if I am around certain girls. My angel taught me how to use my energy to keep their bad influences away from me. Sometimes I dream about things that happen the next day. I used to feel like an alien. Now I have learned that I have gifts—and because of them my life is better.

Nine-year-old Beth described a guardian angel in her life.

> The first five years of my life I was very close to my grandmother. I spent one day a week with her ever since I was born. Those days were spent playing together—any fantasy either one of us chose. No matter how I felt, my grandma was on my side. If some kid was mean to me, she always helped me to feel better. She never criticized me or made me feel stupid. She died when I was five years old. For a long time I felt very sad. I missed her every day. During that first six months after she died, my grandma started appearing to me. Now, four years later, I still know she is nearby. Even when I do not see her, I feel her around me keeping me safe. She is like my guardian angel. Grandma is still around taking care of me—and helping me to grow up!

Jordan, a nine-year-old Catholic girl, hesitantly shared her spiritual experience of having angels and feeling the presence of God.

I have three angels. I don't know if they have names or not.
I know that one of them was my mom's grandfather and the
other was my dad's father. My angels just hang out with me
and help me. They don't talk to me. The time they helped me
the most was when our dad left us for three years and I felt
very sad. Then they helped me again when my grandfather
died and I was there, visiting my father and him. Then there
is God who is with me all the time. When I feel the presence
of God, I feel safer. He is my friend, except even better than
a friend.

Another blessed child was five-year-old Jane. She had disclosed many uncomfortable feelings and confidential experiences to me for more than a year. I was surprised when she said she had something else to say that she had never told me.

Mollie, I have angels who take care of me! There are at least
three of them. They are sixteen—and I guess you'd call them
teenagers. They watch over me! They aren't always together.
Usually they take turns protecting me, one at a time, some-
times for a whole year each turn. Their names are Laurel,
Nicole, and Mallory. Right now Nicole is watching over me. She
has long brown hair and brown eyes. Wait, I have at least four
angels, probably more! I just remembered the other one's
name. It is Christy. They all love me and take turns keeping
me safe from harm.

At seven years old, Sean was a most energetic spiritual kid. He happily told me that most people have angels—that he, in fact, has nine.

Most of my angels are boys. There are six boys and three girls.
The boys don't have halos, but they have stars on their wings.
They have webbed feet, so if I am in water they can swim
after me. They are always beside me, like nine feet away. The
really really strong ones are like really close to me. They pro-
tect me and they give me answers for my problems. They stay
with me all the time. They never go with anyone else. . . .

Mollie, I want to tell you something, but I'm not sure if I should. My brain tells me not to tell you, but my soul tells me it's OK. I had to go to the hospital for tests. It was very embarrassing, because they looked at my privates to give me shots. The doctor and nurses were grouchy and just told me to hold still. When the doctor told me they needed to operate that night, I started to ask questions. The doctor told me to save my questions for after the surgery. I cried. I was very afraid. Then my guardian angels surrounded me and told me they would watch over me and not let anything bad happen. I just felt calmer, and I stopped crying. I wasn't afraid anymore. And everything worked out just fine.

Isabella, an eight-year-old whose mother had died in a car accident, eagerly announced that she had not only one angel but five. She knew that three angels were deceased family or friends. The first was her grandma on her mother's side, another was her great-great-grandma on her dad's side, and the third was the recently deceased mother of a close friend.

Boys and girls often enjoy spiritual companion relationships with deceased persons who do not necessarily present themselves as angels. When I met six-year-old Thomas, he was grieving the recent death of his great-grandmother. In our third session he said she always visits him.

She is happy and wants to be sure that I am safe. When she was living, she told me that I had light bulbs in my head. She said they helped me to have good ideas. I have an imaginary companion who cleaned out my light bulbs this week at one of the Rockies' games.

Faith

Many spiritual children have visitors who are related to their faiths. Katherine, a twelve-year-old Catholic girl with straight A's, was a great athlete and very popular with the kids. She started therapy as a result of her mother's illness. She told the following story.

A couple of years ago the Blessed Virgin Mary began to appear to me on occasion. One afternoon she told me that my mother was sick with cancer. I told no one, but I suffered deeply for my mother and everyone involved. Months later my mother shared the disturbing news with my sister and me.

Four-year-old Colten is a Catholic boy on the fourth branch. During our first time together, he told me,

Mary, Jesus, and God visit me all the time. They come together. Mary knocked at my bedroom door. The first time she came in and laid by me. I showed her my dog because she doesn't have a dog. Mary always talks to me. Last time she told me that she is with me all the time at home; that Jesus and God are always there, too. I feel safe. They all love me. Mary is never sad when I see her. She told me that I am just as cool as my brother. Jesus and God talk to me, too, but I can't remember what they say. This happens a lot. I even know when they will be coming.

Colten continued about his pet that recently died: "Mary let me see my hamster, Buddy. He's alive up in heaven. Animals can come back to earth soon, but people have to take longer." As Colten spoke of his special visitors, he drew one beautiful rainbow after another.

Spiritual Companions

Many children have spiritual companions who are not guardian angels, Jesus, Mary, or God. They are nonetheless important to the child's well-being. Ashley's spiritual companion, Rob, was one of these, while both a protective friend and close partner. With Rob around, Ashley was never too lonely. She always had a helper.

Rob is at school. He is in the first grade, the invisible first grade. He does math. He reads his journal. There's an invisible teacher. Rob comes home with me every day after school. I am going to marry him when I am old enough. Rob's grandma and grandpa and aunt and uncle are going to come live with us. They are nice. Rob helps his grandma make dinner. If I am sad, he comes over and makes me happy again. He sings me a song or reads me a story. He goes to school pretty early. Once we went on a treasure hunt. There was a pirate ship, a pretend one that stole me from him. Rob rescued me.

At other times, boys and girls have actual physical beings that are meaningfully positioned in their lives. Despite many losses, six-year-old Scilla enjoyed a butterfly named Flutterby who was her spiritual buddy. Scilla alluded to this uplifting story of love, friendship, free will, and responsibility.

Mollie, a couple of months after my dad died, I was at school and we had butterflies all around us. They had just hatched in a science experiment. Some of them landed, and some of them flew away. Finally, everyone else's flew away, except for mine. Everyone stayed an extra hour to see if my butterfly would fly away, too. But it didn't want to leave. It just stayed on my shirt or on my hand. So the teacher finally told me I had to take it home. I kept it overnight. It was such a kind butterfly. Then my mom told me that I had to release him. So I did, but he wouldn't leave. He stayed one hour on my shirt, and then he flew into my yard. He went everywhere with me. His name was Flutterby.

Sometimes I saw him in the front yards at neighbors' houses where I was visiting. He was so wonderful. I'll never forget him. Can you believe this amazing story? One time he flew right up to a cobweb. I told him he was going into a time-out if I caught him because if he got stuck in that cobweb, he could have died. I was upset. I was worried about him. He was my responsibility because I was there when he hatched. He chose me, so I had to take care of him. I did not ever want to find out that someone caught him, or he got trapped in a cobweb, or he hit a window, or his wing got ripped. Ever since Flutterby has been in my life, I've known that I would be OK.

Scilla's mother told me that the butterfly story was true. Scilla understood that butterflies usually do not hang around people for

long, that whatever the reasons, her relationship with such a delicate being was very special. Flutterby served to help her feel a deep
and necessary connection, reminding her that despite her grief she
could still know the joy of belonging.

Elves and Fairies

Five-year-old John told the following story of a very special spiritual
companion, "an elf that lives at my house."

> *He sleeps with me at night and hangs out during the day. He
> protects me. When I first saw him, I was scared and asked
> him, "What are you doing here?" He usually visits me at my
> mom's house. My mom says she used to have an elf, too. Our
> elves are brother and sister. Mine is a boy elf. Both of these
> elves hang on trees. I want my elf to write you a letter and
> come to see you sometimes, Mollie. I can't promise that he will,
> but I'll try to convince him. I'm not weird, just because I have
> an elf for a friend, am I?*

Susan was a bright ten-year-old who told of her experiences with
fairies at bedtime.

> *I see dots flying around in my room above my head at night
> when my lights are out. The dots are clear, blue, pink, and
> yellow. They are made by fairies that are on the ceiling drop-
> ping them. There are toys flying around and sometimes some
> jewelry. I gently grab as many of the toys as I can, and I put
> them in my hands. Then I let them all fly away. This usually
> goes on for four hours. Then I fall asleep. Sometimes it hap-
> pens during the day.*

Six-year-old Alex excitedly told me about her fairy.

> *My fairy has on a blue dress, and she has green eyes. She
> has pink wings. She flies a lot. She has brown hair. She lives
> in the grass and her world is called Never Land. She's very
> nice. She likes children, and diamond rings, and crystals.
> She lives by lots of flowers and shady spots. The sun wakes
> her up. She wears blue shoes to match her dress and a little*

crystal on each shoe. She meets lots of friends on her journey. She finds lots of crystals. Her favorite things are dolphins, and when she grows up she wants to be a dolphin trainer. She wants to get married. When I'm sad, she helps me. She says nice things. When I'm mad, she calms me down. She takes care of me, and her name is Sue. She's named after my mommy.

Jenna was a delightful spiritual child. As her trust in me developed, she began to tell me many stories about spiritual companions she called her real friends, accounts similar to those she had disclosed to her parents since she could talk. Asserting that she remembered "growing this old with hundreds of frosted fairies, the ones who have all the powers," she said in a quiet tone,

Anytime we ask our frosted fairies, they bring us to the prettiest thing of all. They bring me to something that is pretty— really beautiful. It is magic, but I won't tell you where the prettiest thing of all is. . . . OK, it's in the heavens! I just saw it. It is the beautifullest thing of all.

I've seen the real God before he was at the church. I remember that time. He looked a lot like my dad with short hair. He had on a cape like a king. The cape was brown. Everyone could see him. There were a lot of people there. I just know where this beautifullest thing is. I have the key to it! Only the fairies know where it is. If you pick up the ring, you'd better not wake my magic up. I have two rings, two golden magic rings. I can see the most beautiful thing of all in the heavens. It is the castle of God! It is like a palace. It's painted pink. When I go to the castle of God, I can walk in there. But you don't have the key to the castle. You can go to the church, but it doesn't have the magic—it's only in the palace!

Twelve-year-old Annie told me about her elf, Johnny, who had lived with her since she could remember. She called him the elf of good and bad, emphasizing that he had been her elf of happiness.

The elves have a king elf that assigns them to children that need their gift. Or the opposite: he assigns the elf to a child

who can teach the elf about goodness. The elves leave the child when the child grows up. Then they are paid. They give all their money to their children, who may number as many as five hundred. Then they are reassigned to a new child. The elves are assigned to babies every time one is born. They live in heaven and they never die.

Many elves, like mine, are mischievous. I told him to stop teasing me and to be clearer about what he was saying. I asked him sternly, "Are you here to help me or not?" He just kept running around and wouldn't answer me, so when I held him down, he cut his chin and it healed immediately with a couple of drops of blood disappearing on the brick. Then he said, "That's why we never die, because as soon as we find out that we are sick or wounded, it heals immediately. You see, Annie, I live in a perfect world. There's no violence like there is here. We're all loving toward each other. When I am assigned to a child, I'm the child's partner. I help the kid to know bad from good. And you, Annie, are here to teach me even more about good and bad."

One-Time Visions

Sometimes spiritual children are exposed to spirits with whom they do not have ongoing relationships, and these isolated incidents are difficult to explain. Ten-year-old Chelsea, from a Christian family, told me an amazing story.

I was lining up for lunch when I saw a little girl with a pink backpack. Her hair was almost to her waist—brown and shiny. She wore tennis shoes with mostly pink on them. She had a ribbon or headband that was also mostly pink in her hair. She wore blue jeans. I couldn't see her eye color. She was walking up the hill on the school grounds about six feet from the memorial tree for five-year-old Christina, a kindergartner who died mysteriously in her sleep. She had missed a week of school with an illness, but she was so much better her mother sent her back to school. After she returned to school for one day, she died that night in her sleep. The cause of her death was unknown.

The reason I noticed her was because no one steps on the ground where the memorial tree is; not even the boys who are troublemakers will go there. The littlest kids at school know better. It's like there's this respect for that tree and the ground around it. This little girl seemed different, like she was just hanging out for a while. She seemed completely comfortable to be by the tree. She kept looking at the street and then the tree memorial. I turned my head for five seconds to tell my friend Meg to look. When I glanced back, she was nowhere to be seen. No one could have disappeared that quickly. I could see the whole area very clearly. I had chills all over me. It was so weird. Everything seemed extra quiet.

Seeing Colors

Many kids on the fourth branch see colors, rainbows, or auras. Rebecca claimed she saw rainbows around people. During her last session with me, after drawing a picture of her rainbow she made a clay image. It included a little girl, obviously overflowing with joy, with one end of the rainbow perched solidly on each shoulder. Rebecca glanced into my eyes as she finished her sculpture, hastily wrapping her arms around my neck to give me one of the bear hugs she usually reserved for her mother. She whispered in my ear, obviously feeling confident, "Mollie, you can keep this present I made for you! I call it the Light of Rebecca."

Seven-year-old Kristina began to see brilliant colors around family members and friends after her father's death. She was pleasantly surprised and grateful to have this spiritual gift. "What colors do I have around me today?" became a fun question her family would ask. Sometimes she volunteered information about a friend whose colors had changed drastically since a visit only a few days previously. Her amazing gift lasted about one and a half years.

Flying

I believe that most children wish they could fly. Many children on the fourth branch say they remember flying; many others have vivid dreams of flying; even more have the intense desire to do so again. Parents become alarmed when their children talk about dreams or memories of flying, but flying reminds children of being in the spirit, free from the confines of their bodies.

Some children become obsessed with the thought of flying and try hard to accomplish it. Ten-year-old Austen had dreams of flying every night and often stated his determination to learn: "I know that I can fly!" Five-year-old Margaret, who injured herself on the playground, intended to fly when she jumped off a platform several feet above the ground.

Seven-year-old Anna told the following story.

Mollie, I wish that I could really fly. I dream about it mostly every night, except for last night because I was too excited about my new guinea pig. When I fly, I go 3,546 miles an hour. I get to see cars, and houses, and birds. I fly faster than the birds. My brother and I both try to fly when we are awake, but we never get the hang of it. We put wings on our arms but nothing ever works. Even though we have only been able to fly in our dreams, I still know that we can actually fly someday.

Natalie was somewhat hesitant to speak. She told me she wanted to pretend that we were twins: "I am magic from the fairy dust in the playroom. I ate it! I want to go flying with you. Before I go today I'll show you how I can fly. Watch me, Mollie; this is how you fly!"

As Natalie launched herself from her platform, her movements were light and quick. She landed only a couple of feet from the table where she began and seemed very pleased with her attempt. It was as though her spirit had become airborne, soaring into the universal flying space of her inner self.

Sean also knew how to fly, saying, "I can't do it anymore because my body is too heavy, but I remember how great it felt when I used to fly. I can still fly in my dreams. I love those times the best of all!"

Scilla remembered that she once was able to fly, and it was inconceivable to her that she would not still have this gift.

I actually know how to fly—you have to have wings that won't flop down like silk wings do. They have to be strong enough to catch the wind. Your wings must be able to flap to push the air down. That's why birds can fly. They have strong enough wings. Anyway, that's how you fly. . . . My hopes of flying will never stop. I'll never give up. I'm hoping someone will make me strong enough wings attached to my arms so I can fly.

Many children have disclosed to me their adventures in the world of spirit: journeys with angels and other spiritual companions; seeing lights, rainbows, and auras around people; and remembering how to fly. They also came to realize the incredible worth of their spiritual gifts that offer them so much richness, joy, and comfort.

What to Know, Say, and Do
for Spiritual Partners on the Fourth Branch

Spiritual kids cannot be happy and healthy while hiding such important parts of themselves as their guardian angels or spiritual companions. Give them ways to announce the presence of these special beings, for instance, by drawing pictures of them. Display these next to their beds or study areas, and share them with trusted friends and family. Animation—or the bringing to life of their worlds with drawings, poems, letters, and discussions—can be the key to children feeling validated and OK about who they are. Make a book with your children to describe their angels in great detail. You can help by questioning, "What are your angels' names? How many are there? What do they look like—boys or girls?" Your task is to communicate such a degree of openness that your spiritual children will feel safe enough to freely pursue the spiritual world, even into adulthood.

Remember that in a world which is often rejecting, spiritual children yearn to be recognized, accepted, and appreciated for their remarkable gifts. Keep in mind that spiritual partners also need confirmation. You, like your younger counterparts, would greatly profit from support groups where you could discuss your discomforts and apprehensions concerning your spiritual boys and girls and, of course, yourselves. Resources for these are cited at the end of this book.

Some spiritual children on the fourth branch will greatly benefit from private schools that allow the child to blossom spontaneously, emphasizing creative abilities that are so closely related to their spiritual gifts. However, in both public and private schools one will discover dedicated teachers who have a deep appreciation for the spiritual wonders of their students. When possible, personally select the individual teacher who has the potential for encouraging your children on their spiritual pathways. Look for many of the same characteristics as are described for therapists and others in the introduction, once again relying on trustworthy referrals.

Remember, it is critical to children's healthy adjustment to have at least one good friend who shares their interests and values. Expose them to a variety of kids so they can find positive and playful connections with other spiritual children.

Appreciate your spiritual children when they are so elegantly in touch with the divine and longing for recognition of their connection to God. Never assume that you have all the answers. Be inspired to look at your own gifts and the possibility of encountering spiritual companions. The willingness to be receptive and nonjudgmental is a crucial attribute of a helpful spiritual partner.

Children on the fourth branch live in a fascinating world of spirit. Despite their wonderful gifts to see the unseen and travel to worlds invisible to most adults, their experiences are often considered unbelievable, or even ridiculous, by the adults in their lives.

While they suffer with this oppression, they may develop poor self-esteem, show signs of anxiety, and even exhibit feelings of hopelessness. If they continue to be distressed for more than three or four weeks, consult with a therapist, who has the skills to connect with your spiritual child.

Confirm your kids' spiritual needs as they inhabit a world of spirit:

- Engage a therapist who is willing to accept unconditionally the child's unseen world.
- Embrace and celebrate the presence of your child's spiritual companions.
- Appreciate that these spiritual friends are irreplaceable resources for any child undergoing the challenges of life.
- Keep a journal of your child's spiritual companions, experiences, and characteristics.
- Encourage your children to keep their own journals.
- Recognize your child's incredible connection to the divine.

Comfort them:

- Support the ways they are blessed in their uniqueness.
- Facilitate their need to have friends who also play in the world of spirit.
- Help them to feel OK about who they are.
- Be available to listen to the stories about their adventures.
- Provide them with a more creatively based school that enhances spirituality, or work closely with the teacher in a more traditional setting.
- Look at your own gifts and spiritual companions.
- Discuss discomforts and apprehensions about your spiritual child with other spiritual partners.

Communicate with them:

- Encourage and explore their imagination and creativity.

- Suggest that they animate, or bring to life, their worlds with drawings, poems, books, letters, and discussions.
- Ask about their angels and spiritual companions.
- Discuss and accept their spiritual nature.
- Never assume you have all the answers.
- Share your stories of adventures in a world of spirit.
- Never argue with your child about feelings or experiences.

Light and Darkness, Good and Evil

The fifth branch of the Spiritual Tree of Life concerns kids' sensitivity to light and darkness, good and evil. As difficult as it is for children on the fourth branch to reveal their involvement in the world of spirit, it is even more challenging for kids on the fifth branch to make known their sometimes frightening battle between good and evil.

Most spiritual kids, somewhere around ages three to ten, play on this branch, seeing the world in terms of superheroes defeating darkness. They identify perversion, destruction, and hate as evil forces they are compelled to overpower. As superheroes they act out these battles at home, in the playroom, and elsewhere. In therapy the drama is often enacted in the sand table, where they usually express strong emotions, or with puppets they use for interaction.

Soldiers, cowboys, and Indians are often their favorite toys, along with a castle for the good guys, who are sometimes the golden knights; black knights, who are considered evil; and a dragon that protects the children. Most kids ask that I play the part of the bad guys since they are not comfortable with that role. Occasionally, a child will insist on assuming the character of the evil ones, darkness, or the like.

As strong as their desire is to create a world of peace, harmony, and goodwill, these spiritual warriors are determined to fight against the forces that may prevent peacemakers like themselves from being successful in healing their personal, as well as their global, family. They design battlefields on which a war between good and evil is fought. These two opposing forces are eventually assimilated into one. Once this level of integration takes place, spiritual kids will describe the evil they were fighting as "defeated," meaning it no longer has power over them.

For some spiritual kids the struggle between good and evil becomes very real. Our job as spiritual partners is to help them know that they are powerful enough to rid themselves of the evil they believe is surrounding them. As they win the battles they create in their play, their world becomes a friendlier place where they feel a growing sense of empowerment and hope. The elements of good and evil are transformed into a dawn that holds within its sublimity both light and darkness. One mother commented, "When my son fought the evil ones for so many months, I felt like there was an actual war being waged for his life. When he finally defeated the forces of evil in his play, his life took a turn for the better in every area."

Patrick

Spiritual kids' battles may represent an unbearable situation in which they are involved, such as kids whose parents are divorcing, especially the highly litigious kind. These boys and girls greatly benefit from acting as formidable spiritual warriors to end all war. Seven-year-old Patrick, whose parents were involved in a conflict-ridden divorce, enacted a war between the farm people he called the evil ones and the castle people he called the good guys. For the most part, the good guys, at least symbolically, won over the evil ones, who were ultimately destroyed.

Patrick, like other kids who wage war between darkness and light, created a powerfully healing energy. While initially fraught with conflict, this spiritual force is revitalizing, touching the world in much the same way as the energy created by prayer. The two opposing ends of the continuum must first battle before coming together as life-sustaining forces. Despite the minuscule scope of one child's play such as Patrick's, it is one significant battle added to hundreds of others that eventually may have impact on the overall transformation and blending of dark and light, evil and good for the world.

No matter how small, this symbolic war actually functions to soften the harshness of the originally disparate forces. While your spiritual children say, "I have defeated the evil ones," you can understand their statement as meaning that they have reconciled these two forces inside of themselves until they have reached a place of peace. Any objective darkness will have minimal power over such children who have achieved a high level of integration along these lines.

Alyssa

Sometimes the evil that boys and girls on the fifth branch are fighting is symbolic of someone or something that has set out to destroy them. Alyssa, a six-year-old girl, was brought to therapy by her divorced parents because she had been sexually abused by a member of her extended family. Alyssa used puppets several times, referring to the spider puppet as the evil one who made the kitty puppets do "naughty things." Alyssa was the wolf that represented good and eventually destroyed the spider.

In a later session, again as the good wolf, Alyssa prevented "all the horrible evil monster puppets from hurting the children." As her therapy progressed, she asked me to play Junior, a furry arm puppet with an obnoxious and mean personality, as the evil person who had hurt her. She was a girl puppet who played the part of good that fights to win over Junior. Alyssa asserted herself by repeatedly yelling "No!" to Junior. As Alyssa's spiritual partner, her father helped her to defeat Junior; good once again won over evil. By symbolically integrating the darkness and light to which she had been exposed, Alyssa transformed a world that had been colored by abuse, powerlessness, shame, and chaos, and she expanded her sense of personal power and regained her dignity as a spiritual child.

Megan

Megan, brought into therapy by her divorced mother, was fearful of all men and was not comfortable visiting her father. She created a puppet show about Mrs. Unicorn, the twin kitties she named Erin and Sarah Bunny, a Cat That Nobody Likes (later named Ashley), a Devil Guy, and a Policeman. She described their interaction: "All are nice girls, except the Devil is a boy who is trying to hurt the girls and scares them, until the Policeman stops him." Megan made the point that even though the Policeman is a man, he is still good. She knows that lots of men are good. The kitties act surprised when they hear what she says. At the end of the puppet play, Megan has Mrs. Unicorn and Policeman "take care of the evil Devil Guy" after they put him away in a dungeon.

Bobby

Sometimes the evil that boys and girls on the fifth branch are fighting is both symbolic of someone or something that has set out to destroy them and represents an unbearable situation they have experienced. Bobby's story is one of these. He was a three-year-old spiritual child who nearly drowned in a lake where his family was vacationing. Bobby was with a group of children taking swimming lessons; a water-safety instructor and a lifeguard were also present. Other children were already swimming with their families in the area. No one noticed Bobby moving to deeper water. As he began to struggle to stay above the water, for several minutes no one came to his assistance. Finally, his mother, who was swimming a few yards away, felt an overwhelming sense of urgency. When she looked toward the new swimmers and their instructor, she panicked when she did not see her son.

She swam quickly toward the group and found Bobby a few feet away, struggling to stay above the water. By the time she rescued him with the help of other parents, his lips were blue and he was not responding, but within seconds he began to sputter and cough.

On that day Bobby had a near-death experience he did not share for more than a year. He was tormented by his awareness that no one, with the exception of his mother, noticed his distress. His feelings of abandonment were tantamount to death itself. He was no longer a happy-go-lucky child. He did not feel safe anywhere. He suffered severe episodes of stomach pain. Although medication reduced the physical discomfort, he responded with intense crying episodes. He began to put himself at risk, such as climbing to the tops of trees. Once he tied a belt around his neck and exclaimed to his mother, "Mom, I want to die!" It was as though Bobby were tempting fate.

Bobby clung to his mother when it was time to attend kindergarten; eventually, his parents withdrew him from school. Although he had had many friends, he no longer felt close to them, nor did he expend energy to make new ones. He changed from a child who had a deep love for animals to a boy who treated pets with anger and distrust. He often made statements describing his distressful feelings such as, "I am such a failure!" or "If you do not trust someone, you're dead."

When Bobby was five years old, during his spiritual journey with me he would dramatize the events of his near-drowning with metaphors, spending most of his time in the sand table running his hand through the sand as though it were water. He would bury dozens of cowboy figurines head first, saying they were dead. He would then bury the rest of the soldiers and all the Indians as he announced loudly, "The cowboys and Indians are pulling each other under!" As an Indian pushed a cowboy under the sand, he yelled, "You will never come back, cowboy, because there's a tornado under there!"

As Bobby felt more comfortable with me, he disclosed the story of his spiritual visitors, both at a cemetery and at the lake. A few weeks earlier, after his grandpa had died, Bobby saw ghosts and monsters at the cemetery. During his play session, he drew the cemetery.

There are ghosts, and goblins, and monsters, and rats, and mice in some cemeteries. There are 101 of them in my grandpa's cemetery. I know, because I saw them! I saw ghosts, goblins, and monsters at the cemetery the day my grandpa died after he had a heart attack. The ghosts, goblins, and monsters wanted to meet me. They came toward me and knocked me down. I was not scared of any of them, because I smacked them, too!

For many months Bobby repeated his themes of submersion, death, rebirth, and, most significantly, victory over the forces of darkness. Once he played in the dollhouse for a few minutes before he quickly moved back to the sand table, where he grabbed buried Indians. Removing them from their sand grave, he carried them back to the dollhouse with great enthusiasm. "Now the Indians have a place to live!" Bobby was dramatizing his inner healing with the Indians who, like himself, at first were drowning but by now had found a place of safety.

Bobby often pretended to be suffocating, having several heart attacks, and drowning. One day, many weeks after our first meeting, he pretended that he had died by shooting himself in the head. When he began to breathe again, he said that when he almost drowned he was not only dead but had been visiting dead people, adding that he had not seen his grandpa among them. Although he remembered almost drowning and his mother saving him with the help of a lifeguard, this was the first time he alluded to his near-death experience.

After that he would often describe his near-drowning: "I only died for a minute or two, and then I came back with the living. Now I am really alive!" He would explain that his experience involved contact with spirits who battled one another for his life.

Each spirit had a different job. The good spirits were there to save me, so I could be with my family. The evil or black spirits wanted to drag me deeper and deeper into the water, until I no longer would belong to this world!

Bobby feared that the spirits might tear him in two as they struggled against one another. During the short time he was close to death, he believed it was imperative that he voice a decision whether to live or die.

Under Bobby's direction, the puppets representing good and bad fought with one another.

Mollie, I killed all the mean and powerful monsters and skeletons that were trying to drown me. I killed all the bad guys who were pulling me under the water and not letting me go back up out of the water. I needed the wizard's help, at first.

As Bobby played out the war of good versus evil, he gradually decided that the bad puppets would change—not only into good puppets but into his friends as well. He singled out the powerful skeleton figure, a part of his frightening journey. "I believe that the skeleton is so strong, I need my friend the frog to agree to kill him. I am too weak." Even though the frog did not like killing anything, Bobby would speak for him, "I will kill the skeleton for you since you do not believe that you can do it by yourself!"

I recommended that Bobby become part of a play group, hoping they would offer support to one another by telling of their frightening experiences. Each time they met, however, Bobby would become very ill. As he begged his parents not to make him go, he would say with tears in his eyes, "I am not like the other kids!" Bobby was hungering for a connection with children who had similar experiences. Therefore, I read him *Closer to the Light: Learning from the Near-Death Experiences of Children*, by Melvin Morse. For the first time, he began to feel that he truly was not alone in his pain—that he was not strange or crazy. His enthusiasm during that session was remarkable.

Bobby continued to play with me only for a few more weeks until finally he no longer needed my support. He attended school and made friends and good grades while he celebrated his incredible transformation. He gradually found inner peace, strength, and vitality as he assimilated these opposing forces into one.

Jeremy

Occasionally, I meet children who spend most of their time fighting the forces of evil. Rare even among spiritual children, these kids feel they are on a mission to save the world from the forces of darkness. Their desire to help others may show itself at a very young age. Parents will report that sometimes their children speak of feeling the presence of evil outside their therapeutic playrooms, at home and at school, sometimes even in their churches; they feel actual outside forces that they are compelled to engage in battle. Although all the kids on the fifth branch are spiritual warriors, these exceptional boys and girls, who are also astutely aware of the presence of God or goodness, are crusaders in the purest sense of the word.

They are champions of their cause: to rid the world of evil while promoting peace. Their war, as they describe it, is the same battle between darkness and light described earlier in this chapter. However, their role as a spiritual warrior originates from deep within them—at times present almost since birth—rather than as the result of an identifiable hurtful person or situation that may create inner conflict. It is crucial that they fight to the finish, until there is a blending or integration of the two forces. As they celebrate their victory, these children realize inner and outer peace.

Jeremy is one of these rare children. He was absorbed in a mission to defeat the forces of darkness. Starting on his unique spiritual journey at two years old, as soon as he was able he spoke clearly. "I am here," he would say, "to teach people. I teach everyone!" Jeremy's parents were speechless. His mother, without having the words to describe her son's uncanny sensitivity and wisdom, knew that Jeremy was an especially spiritual child—a life she remembered as a child and still glimpsed many years later.

When I met Jeremy, now five years old, he appeared to be extremely bright and assertive. He took great effort to portray his feelings, convictions, and struggles, using many sophisticated words to tell his stories, especially of his parents' recent divorce. After he felt safe with me and knew I would be unconditionally supportive no matter how disturbing his enactments, he disclosed a frightening part of his spiritual play journey—his battle with darkness, or the "evil ones," as he called them.

In the playroom Jeremy relentlessly fought the dark forces for six months. During that time he desperately needed my backing as well as the continued support of his parents and siblings to rid his world of all evil spirits. Jeremy's mother also "played" in the playroom. Jeremy often took over the role of the evil one in his puppet play while he slammed around the mom puppet.

Hoping to save herself, his mother handcuffed the evil puppet as she gradually became more effective in her efforts to fight him. In response to his mother's newfound strength, Jeremy insisted on handcuffing her and assigned himself to be a "number two evil one" to help "battle against the goodness in Mom." Jeremy would then handcuff himself as he handcuffed his mother, shouting, "Leave, devil!" and then quickly commanding, "No, evil one, before you leave make Jeremy cry first!" At that point he would look pleadingly into my eyes and say, "My mother and I are losing the battle with the evil ones!"

One day Jeremy made a special request: "Now I want to bury my body in the sand! Then after I am buried, I will fight the evil ones! I will be the strongest! But first, I need to put sand all over me!" Covering most of his body except his head, Jeremy was extremely pleased with himself. It was as though the grains were baptismal waters—at the same time cleansing and strengthening his spirit so he might shine forth to "teach all people" lessons of love. He exclaimed, "That feels just right! Tell my mom, please, Mollie! Go get her, and let her see what I am doing! Then I will fight the evil ones once again!"

Jeremy's battle against evil appeared to be a matter of life or death for him. Eventually, he announced that he had defeated the strongest "evil one," the skeleton. Many weeks later Jeremy realized that he had won the battle once and for all. He celebrated his rebirth as he remembered the day the "real Jeremy boy" built the castle with his mother's help. He played that a baby egg, representing Jeremy, was hatching, giving birth to a little bird. He began to make flowers and bugs out of modeling clay such as Play-Doh, inviting his mother to join him. With great delight he gave his mother two flowers. He said of the larger, more colorful flower, "This is the Jeremy flower because it is wide open and blooming. Now I'm free and I can take the stars and put them in my eyes, and my eyes sparkle, and all of me sparkles!"

Jeremy was beginning to find inner peace by winning his spiritual battle. The changes were unmistakable. He became calmer, happier, and more carefree while still insisting, "I am here to teach others!" He was more assertive with his sisters and expressed his feelings and needs. His family and friends began to respond to him more positively. Jeremy was learning to love and accept himself as a good person deserving of happiness. He was moving out of his grief concerning his parents' divorce. Most significant, in his play and at home, church, and school he was no longer tormented by the presence of the evil ones.

Spiritual children who play on this fascinating branch are extraordinary human beings who deserve our attention, respect, acceptance, and protection. Although fighting evil is sometimes a frightening concept, spiritual partnership demands that we are dauntless in our support of these young crusaders who so lovingly touch our world.

What to Know, Say, and Do
for Spiritual Partners on the Fifth Branch

Boys and girls playing on the fifth branch of the Spiritual Tree of Life are extremely sensitive to the notion of light and darkness and good and evil, creating battlefields in their play where they defeat the evil ones. They are healers at heart. If they are to comfortably contribute their gifts to the world, they must have the unconditional support of spiritual partners. They desperately need such partners not only to believe in and understand their intense journeys but also to communicate their understanding compassionately.

As spiritual partners you must realize there is no branch that more urgently requires your unconditional acceptance and nonjudgmental presence. Although your children's ultimate goal is to promote peace and love in the world, without your backing during encounters with the evil ones they are likely to feel overwhelmed, alone, and unprotected. They may even lose the necessary courage to engage in these battles, and if they find it impossible to identify and safely express their feelings—especially anger—it will create in them resentfulness, dishonesty, and defiance. Ultimately, the trust in your relationship will erode.

Once again when your spiritual children say, "I have defeated the evil ones," translate their statement as meaning that they have come to peace with two opposing forces inside themselves. Any objective darkness will have little or no power over these highly integrated children.

Give these boys and girls opportunities to be leaders! Watch their cues regarding where leadership may shine, such as at school, at church, or in scouts. For instance, perhaps encourage them to be junior journalists to begin to send their messages to the world.

When your children say the battle with evil is over, celebrate like you've never celebrated before! Commemorate the delightful statements they make as they move into the light after such an intense time of darkness. Make banners, cards, or scrapbooks of their journeys. Write key words on a special cake, or on cookies, or on a poster board, triumphantly announcing, "Now I'm free!" And have them journal and draw as they rejoice in their victory.

Spiritual boys and girls who have had near-death experiences are unique. They often also play on several branches, such as the fourth in the world of spirit, the sixth involving healing play often through metaphor, and the seventh of spiritual transformation. If your children have had close calls with death, it is likely they had significant spiritual journeys of which they are hesitant or unwilling to speak. They may likely feel that something is wrong with them and desperately need your help. Whether they tell their stories about near-death experiences with words or symbolically in their play, you need to acknowledge them as courageous kids. Encourage them with such statements as, "You went on a very special journey. You have great courage! It wasn't easy for you to tell me, or anyone." Listen to their stories with an open heart and mind. Several authors who work closely with children have described such near-death experiences. I have listed some of those books in the resource section of this book.

Be sure that all spiritual children who are sensitive to the notion of darkness are given puppets or stuffed toys ("stuffies") that symbolize the strength of the good they so deeply desire. Such representatives of good will help them feel safe at every moment, even while asleep.

Children on the fifth branch need your unconditional support of their battle between good and evil, light and darkness. If your encouragement does not alleviate their intense focus on the presence of evil within a few weeks, consult with a therapist who is spiritually aware.

Confirm your kids' spiritual needs as they fight the forces of darkness:

- Identify and empathize with their sensitivity to the notion of light and darkness.
- Teach them they are healers at heart, here to promote peace and love in the world.
- Believe in their intense journeys.
- Realize there is no branch on which they play that more urgently requires your unconditional love and nonjudgmental presence.
- Give them opportunities to be leaders, and watch for clues regarding where their leadership may shine.

Comfort them:
- Stand with them during encounters with darkness, whether you believe the encounters are metaphorical or literal.
- Help them to overcome being defiant, indirect, or dishonest when expressing feelings, especially anger.
- Give them something representative of the good they so deeply desire, such as puppets or "stuffies" that will help them feel safe at all times, even while asleep.

Communicate with them:
- Compassionately communicate your understanding of the realness and importance of their mission.
- Validate their purpose on earth.
- Translate their statement "I have defeated the evil ones" as meaning that they have come to peace with two opposing forces inside themselves.
- Help them to understand that any objective darkness will have little or no power over them as they become highly integrated children.

Healing Play

6

While balanced on the fifth branch of the Spiritual Tree of Life, children promote peace and goodness by engaging in spiritual warfare and triumphing over forces of evil. On the sixth branch, they become more generally focused on play that heals whatever distresses them.

For nearly twenty years children on the sixth branch have been teaching me about the amazing benefits of healing play. It is their language. As such they communicate their feelings and life experiences, and this language is similar to how adults use words to describe who they are, where they have been, and what they think and feel. However, spiritual kids' colorful play on the sixth branch is more than verbal expression or descriptions of their inner world. It is their participation in unseen worlds—as though they are enraptured by a reality that transports them out of their everyday awareness.

Often, spiritual children's stories are metaphorical. They represent a message, idea, situation, or person in an indirect, symbolic way. The same wisdom arises when they participate in the creative process of healing play. As they travel through symbolic territory, their newly woven experiences are felt to be as authentic as the trauma they have experienced in the so-called real world of the adult. The fact that their stories are real to them is an immense resource as they go about transforming their sometimes troubled worlds.

Dylan

Dylan added powerful elements to soften his traumatic story. Like so many other spiritual kids, he spent time with me as his spiritual partner creating metaphorical stories about his life, especially the more heartrending aspects. For example, he often played that we got in the car, put on our seatbelts—which he called "safety suits"— and drove the furry arm puppet Freddie to the zoo. This trip was a reenactment of his traumatic outing with his mother when their car rolled five times. However, while wearing these suits it was impossible for us to be injured, and in the presence of his spiritual partner, his anxiety created by the accident was greatly reduced. As he added these components of safety to his story, Dylan was no longer fearful that he would be hurt in another accident.

Most children are completely absorbed in healing play that commands all their interest and attention. These are the kids who never want to leave the playroom. Nothing is important enough to distract them from their play. As they become totally engaged they move inward, raising themselves to a place in which their healing powers are magnified. It is in this state that they are their wisest, freest, and most balanced selves.

Mandy

Eight-year-old Mandy was involved in healing play as a result of poor self-esteem. Starting in kindergarten she was easily overwhelmed by details, would often lose the big picture, and had difficulty with fine motor skills. As a result, she was involved in occupational therapy for a couple of years with children many of whom, unlike Mandy, were very distressed with much more severe problems. Consequently, Mandy, who was a very intelligent, perceptive, and securely attached girl, felt that there was something terribly wrong with her if she needed the same classes in which these children were involved. When her parents suggested that she come to my playroom, she was skeptical that this new therapy would be good for her. She only felt that she was "once again not measuring up."

As Mandy's new therapist, I knew I was going to need help, so I called on the expertise of the playroom's lovable, soft, and fuzzy monkey puppet Freddie to help Mandy build trust in herself and me. When he attempted to eat Mandy's shoes, she laughed readily, offering them to him for his dinner. Within the playful framework of this relationship, Mandy felt complimented that Freddie was so comfortable with her, wanting to play and laugh, and obviously liking her so much. As the weeks passed, she developed a relationship with Freddie that was a starting point for her to feel good about herself. Her self-esteem and trust improved markedly over a short period of time.

Healing play is often based on the child's relationship with a variety of puppets, dolls, and figurines, as well as the therapist. In some cases, especially concerning issues of self-esteem, a child will gravitate to the most playful and nurturing puppet in the playroom, such as Freddie, who never fails to be entertaining. In the presence of an unconditionally accepting other, the child client feels liked and accepted. Girls and boys on this branch will redefine who they are in the light of recognition and approval. Their self-esteem will take a turn for the better almost immediately.

Angie

Six-year-old Angie was a child who had been sexually abused. As she played with Freddie, the furry arm puppet, she added him to her repertoire of resources. She taught him that she needed to learn about the importance of feeling safe and about how to say no. She explained that he can trust some people and not others. She brought the dragon puppet to life as her perpetrator, "a monster that came at night and destroyed everyone. When the dragon comes, people are only safe if they are in their homes with their moms." Enlisting the help of Freddie, she then decided that the dragon must be destroyed. As Freddie, whom she trusted and loved, accommodated her by destroying her metaphorical perpetrator, her healing play came full circle.

Spiritual kids use healing play adventures so their once distressful worlds will transform into a place where they can eventually enjoy harmony, dignity, and empowerment. The creative elements they add may include new storylines and outcomes, such as Angie's dragon that Freddie destroyed. These additions are experienced as real parts of their world that lessen the sting of their trauma while increasing their sense of protection and safety. As a result, their experiences are subtly softened to more balanced and nonthreatening versions, especially in the presence of spiritual partners who are nurturing, compassionate, and empathetic participants.

Emily

Six-year-old Emily, whose mother had kidnapped her from her father and had taken her to Canada, insisted that Matt, her father and spiritual partner, join her in healing play. Emily often directed Matt to play the role of the man who tirelessly seeks out his daughter— using the metaphorical character of a shop owner who searches the world for lost pets.

There is a good man who sells pets. He is a dad. Then there are new owners who destroy the house and steal all the pets. He sees a flying truck and follows it. When the truck crashes, the man finds the pets. He says he'll take all the pets home together. The pets speak to the good man, "While you were looking for us, another man stole your daughter. He tied her up and put a piece of tape on her mouth." The dad quickly saved his daughter, saying, "How do you feel, little girl?" She answered, "I feel very bad, because that man gave me a shot in my head." The dad is angry with the mean man. They all go to the hospital and the doctor takes the poison out of the girl's head. It takes ten days. The doctor said, "In ten days she will be better. She won't be sick ever again the rest of her life."

After many arduous sessions, Emily spontaneously insisted that Matt and I be part of a spiritual cleansing ritual or baptism of sorts. She directed us to put our arms in the sand table. She took buckets of sand and slowly poured them over our arms and hands, as though anointing us with healing waters, and she demonstrated how she had washed away the devastation of her past. At the same time she wanted to offer a similar purification or blessing to each of us, who had stood by her as her spiritual partners. As she formally pronounced our names, she wished us happiness, love, peace, and God's blessings. While she performed the ritual with intensity and sincerity, I felt I had indeed been purified by her sacred metaphorical ceremony. Her father and I felt her joy.

Meg

At five years of age, Meg was determined to overcome her fear of shots. She had panicked at the doctor's office when the nurse had unsuccessfully attempted to update her immunizations. She chose the doctor's bag to begin her healing play. She insisted that a couple of the baby dolls, three puppets, and I be her patients, and she repeatedly gave us shots. I interacted with her as if I was a child who was scared of shots—but also one who could be eventually reassured.

Meg comforted us with statements such as, "This will not hurt for long. I will be very gentle with you. Be brave. I know it is very scary to get a shot." For several sessions, she moved about the room like Florence Nightingale on a mission. After immunizing each of us a number of times, Meg was ready to face her own fears. The next time I met with her she announced proudly that, although hesitant, she had allowed her family physician to give her the shots she needed.

Jonathan

In his healing play, Jonathan chose metaphorical themes to disclose his journey of struggle and triumph. He communicated the anguish he felt about many unresolved and disturbing issues, such as being sexually and emotionally abused by his babysitter and grieving the loss of his baby sister, who died at birth. In his play he was a super-hero who conquered many aspects of his abuse, at times becoming a shark that would viciously attack, kill, and consume any intruders in order to keep him safe. He displayed his outrage at the injustices in his life by stating,

> *When bees get stomped on, they lose their life. Careless people stomp on them. Then a nice boy comes along and picks a bee up, and he gets stung. Sometimes I hurt myself, because I am afraid that I killed my sister. I didn't want her to be here, and then she died!*

Jonathan played with Todd, the fox puppet. "The fox has a sister who died! She was the smallest in the litter." Devastated by a sense of overwhelming guilt, he was sickened by the thought of his sister's death being, even in the slightest, his fault. He drew a picture of a boy vomiting into the mouth of a puppet. Then he pretended that the boy's nose bled, and the boy's eyes turned a bright red as Jonathan ran to the trash can, dramatically playing that he was vomiting in it.

As Jonathan unearthed the sources of turmoil in his life, he played out the final and complete destruction of his perpetrator by burying his babysitter in the sand. He repeatedly poured boiling soup on her and flushed her down the toilet. Then, talking in baby talk, he made pizza, exclaiming, "I am making Mollie pizza! There you go! It's Mollie pizza!"

Eventually, in his play Jonathan transformed his inner world into a safe place that did not contain the power of a perpetrator and where he was not haunted by the belief that he was responsible for his sister's death. Finding healing in his play, he no longer lived fearfully and self-destructively as a victim. He discovered the creative resources within him to symbolically destroy the woman who had abused him, simultaneously replacing her with the safe, protective nurturance of "Mollie pizza."

Sammy

Sammy had been left to cope with an unbearable heartache since the suicide of his father. He metaphorically surrounded himself with scary notions about dying. He created a story with a group of skiers; he was one of the scouts.

Mollie, I'm scouting ahead to see if there are any other dangers. I found an army tank approaching from out of the ground. I am digging a really deep hole around the army tank. Look, the tank is falling into the hole. It is covered by dirt and giant boulders. Now I am digging a hole around the bad guy, and he will fall into it. Only his helmet is showing. Mollie, I must call 9-1-1 right away. I have to find a safe place where I can be, where I will not die!

After a couple of sessions he disclosed,

This is a story by Sammy. The witch in it is you, Mollie. This is chapter 1. Once upon a time there was a witch and she had two brooms, a magical one and a dull one. She flew around on her magical broom, and she swept away pretty pretty bugs with her dull broom. She had a yellow cat, and the cat bobbed his head up and down.

Sammy glanced up as though checking out my reaction to his witch story about me. I smiled, delighted with his metaphor. Sammy relaxed as he continued.

Now, here is chapter 2. The witch was nice. She never did spooky or scary things. She helped people with their problems. She was happy when they were OK and sad when people were not OK. These people could be anyone in the world. This story reminds me of my dad, because he was not OK.

For many months Sammy courageously faced his fears, feelings of abandonment, and the sadness that saturated his entire being. It was only then that he realized his scariest feeling of all: intense anger that he had toward himself for causing his father's death by thinking and saying hurtful things to both his parents. As Sammy played in the sand, he began to throw the boy figurine, which represented him, from one corner to the next. Then he buried him under several buckets of sand. As he gently distributed the last handful almost motionlessly onto the hill, he lay down in the sand, covering the boy's burial place. He was so still that he appeared to be barely breathing. Then he started to cry. He confessed, in between sobs, that he believed it was his fault his dad had died.

When I saw Sammy a week later, he communicated to me through metaphor that he still did not feel his life was predictably safe. However, he had forgiven himself for the angry things he had said to his parents.

> *I am safe if I hide under a dirt pile in a little tank thing. I'll let my friend into my tank, where he will be safe, too. It is raining so much it floods and everyone dies, except me and my friend. It floods the place for many hours, covering everything except the sticks. No man is in sight!*

Sammy feared he would drown, alone in his sorrow. He was lost on his journey through the wastelands of grief, searching endlessly for any sanctuary, "even under a dirt pile in a little tank thing."

After shooting everything in the playroom with an imaginary gun, Sammy maimed a couple dozen animal crackers, pretending they were real. He removed an eye, ear, mouth, arm, or leg, leaving each one powerless. Then he shot into each one's mouth and face, much like his father had done to himself. The animals would turn into small pieces and be swallowed by a giant. Then he would blast another toy in the head many times, calling him a dummy because he was incapable of feeling any discomfort while Sammy's grief was overwhelming.

In his play, he compared his life to drowning in quicksand because it was such an insidious way to die—slowly taking with it any semblance of life and hope.

> *The dinosaur and some soldiers are in the big hill of quicksand. Even a bird goes flying overhead and gets caught up in the sand. Even another little soldier dies in the sand! . . . But one day the sand got all blown up, and everything got free! The dinosaur survived the quicksand! He walked right out of the pit spitting out the extra sand. His heart was broken, but he was alive!*

After so many months of sadness, Sammy was letting me know that he, too, was coming alive.

Rebecca

Healing play creates a powerful energy, often compelling spiritual partners to take more active roles in their children's lives. Rebecca expressed through metaphor her need for her dad to be more involved in her life.

The puppy is sad because she has been stranded. Her mother is looking for her. When she finds her, the puppy tells her mom that her daddy does not love her. So the mother tells her to do fun things with him, like play catch. The girl and her dad are playing catch when the dad says abruptly, "I've got to go to a meeting!" The puppy cries and says, "I feel bad and sad when you pay no attention to me, Dad!" The father leaves, despite the pleas from the puppy. Then the puppy writes a letter to her own dad, telling him she wants him to show her he loves her by doing things together with her.

Then Rebecca played with the doggie puppet, giving the puppet all the things Rebecca needed: food, affection, and discipline. Then she expressed her strongest sentiment.

The worst thing that can ever happen to anyone is to be ignored! The puppy was sad and lonely when she was not being listened to or fed. When I am ignored, I feel like a robot. When you listen to my stories, I feel like a real person!

Through Rebecca's healing metaphorical play, her father became acutely aware of her distress over his extended absences. As a result he opened his heart, as well as his schedule, to her. Their closeness evolved into a bond of love, freedom, and support.

Jenna

Four-year-old Jenna gradually described the turmoil she felt over the breakup of her family and how tenuously she held on to a sense of safety during the rough transition of her parents' highly conflicted divorce. During that time it was as though she were watching her family be devoured by forces beyond her control. As an incredible child with great wisdom, Jenna played in a world of healing metaphors that told her story. "Mollie, this is the swan family. Here is the mom, dad, boy, and little girl." She quickly grabbed the wolf puppet, which began to devour all the swans. "Mollie, the alligator will save all the swan family, but he will only do it once, not twice!" Then Jenna played with the alligator puppet, ferociously scaring away the wolf. Because the wolf was not discouraged, he returned for his swan dinner. Jenna yelled with alarm, "This time the alligator will not stop him! Look, Mollie! He is killing the whole family of swans!"

While Jenna lived with a fear that she would lose everyone important to her, her metaphorical play was often accented by themes of death and rebirth.

Today I am the baby unicorn who has lost her mommy and daddy. I found them after a long time! Then I am a baby unicorn born again as their new baby unicorn. From then on the baby always sleeps by her mommy!

Jenna was closest to the horse puppet she pretended she would soon lose. She gathered up the animals, announcing that they were all moving. She said to the horse as she handcuffed it, "Horsie, we are selling you!" The horse cried mournfully. Jenna continued harshly,

Even though I love you the mostest, I must handcuff you. Then I will sell you and send you away. There, go now! Horsie is my best friend, and the wolf killed her. I did not let Bear Bear ride on her or even touch her, but the wolf killed Bear Bear, too. Now I'll be your pet—your horse. You're a little girl and your mommy died. There are dangers all around, so we get in the safe barn. Then my favorite horse leaves and dies. I find her dead.

Jenna expressed her appreciation for transition from death to rebirth, exclaiming, "Then, she comes back to life!"

While Jenna feared losing everyone she loved, she was also apprehensive that her spiritual life would be destroyed.

Rain will get our horns out of magic. The rain is killing me. My horn is getting out of magic. I am dying! The baby unicorn is telling me to go to the hospital. I am sad, because I know that I will be forced to sell either the horse or the unicorn.

Kaye

Kaye was a three-year-old girl who shared her parents' fear of dogs. Fortunately, in her healing play she transferred this fear to a couple of the furry arm puppets in the playroom as well as to a dog puppet. She insisted that they not stay in the playroom with us but be taken out to her parents in the waiting room. Together we delivered the "scary puppets" to her mother and father. I directed them to carry on a conversation in their daughter's presence with each of the puppets, making them promise that they would never scare or harm Kaye.

As her parents became familiar with the puppets, Kaye noted that they were enjoying forgiveness, caring, warmth, and safety in their relationship with them. On the other hand, Kaye spent much of her time with the puppets yelling at them, occasionally hitting them, and constantly setting comfortable boundaries between the puppets and her. For example, the puppy puppet said to Kaye, "My friends and I are big and mean and can hurt you." Kaye would respond, scolding the puppet, "You're very mean, and because of that I will never be your friend, and neither will any other kids. *And* you can never play with my toys! *And* I will always hit you and kick you and give you food that makes you sick!"

Next the puppets would make excuses for their "mean ways" in a whiny tone, saying, "Alright, we're sorry, but we just can't be nice. We've tried, but it's too hard to be good!" As the puppets continued to soften in their approach to Kaye, they would regretfully admit that their behaviors were not appropriate and subsequently ask for Kaye's forgiveness so that they could be friends. "Kaye, please forgive us. We'll try harder next time!"

From this healing play Kaye began to feel empowered. She discovered a newfound trust as she was prepared to consider not only the animal puppets but all animals as her friends and no longer a threat to her.

Allison

Using only a few words, Allison drew a picture of a teenage boy and wrote her name on him. Then she acted out two war parties that killed all but one of the soldiers. She smiled in relief after demolishing most of the fighting men. Then she said that the boy who molested her was named Timothy. She clearly expressed her anger in her play by doing "all kinds of bad things to Timothy, killing him, bombing him, hitting him with the bat, punching him in the nose, slapping him, and finally, cutting his privates off!"

The next time I saw Allison, she said that Timothy had tried to rape her when she was five years old. She described many distressing details, explaining that she had never told either of her parents the whole story. Then, like most spiritual children, after engaging in conflict she became involved in a constructive intimacy-building metaphor, such as bringing order to the playhouse. For her peace of mind, it was imperative that she finish her play with a healing story of belonging to home and family as opposed to the destruction she had known as a little girl of five.

Nick

Nick made every effort to engage my attention each time he came into the playroom. For months after his parents' separation following domestic violence he had witnessed, he brought one of his stuffed toys for me to meet and hold. He played out his withdrawal from a distressful world to a safe place by building a wolf's den, explaining, "Mollie, this is my home!" He asked the baby dinosaur, "Please bring me some food and find my family. I want to see my dad, mom, brother, and baby sister." Then for nearly thirty minutes he literally howled like a wolf. "I am a mad and sad he-wolf! Stay away, Freddie!" Suddenly he grabbed Freddie and bit him. Freddie cried while Nick howled louder and longer. Eventually, he demonstrated his need for a spiritual partner by inviting me to be a he-wolf: "You are another wolf like me. You have to take care of me. You make a fire for me. You cook for me. You howl with me."

Although Nick's basic nature was gentle, caring, loving, and hopeful, he found himself in a dark and scary place, alone without faith that things would ever be good again. So that I would understand the distress he felt, in his healing play he tied me up and said,

> *You must stay in the dark, where crocodiles will scare you and eat your shoes, and a real monkey will tickle you. Then the ghosts will eat your shirt, and Pokey sticks will hurt your nose! There is a cave that is really dark and spooky. You will live there next. No one else lives there, but it is there all the time.*

Over the months as Nick confronted his tormenting fears and dreadful feeling of being alone, he began to believe there was hope for a much better tomorrow. The emotional walls he had constructed, which blocked his ability to give and receive love, came tumbling down.

Rose

Boys and girls on the sixth branch are open to their families' often unexpressed heartaches. As spiritual sponges, their stories are sometimes based literally on unrevealed traumas that may have occurred many generations earlier rather than on metaphorical descriptions. They soak up the distress of their families and communities and begin to act out in upsetting ways. Their parents become concerned and often seek professional help for them. Subsequently, while engaged in healing play the kids unknowingly expose the distressful stories as narratives they have spontaneously created. When the issues are finally exposed, they help bring closure, eventually moving everyone involved to a place of greater awareness, positive change, and peace.

In the dollhouse Rose repeatedly depicted the story of a young man who died in a fire. After a couple of weeks of play, she added that the woman who was watching the fire was finally able to say good-bye to the man. When I shared my confusion about the story with Rose's mother, her eyes suddenly lit up although she appeared both shocked and awestruck.

I'm not sure what this could be about, except that when I was about six years old, my sixteen-year-old brother went to sleep while smoking in his bed and he burned the house down, killing himself. I've always regretted the fact that I never said good-bye to my brother! But Rose knows nothing about this!

Although Rose knew of the recent death of another uncle, she had never been told that he had died from carbon monoxide poisoning in his car while in his garage. However, two months after I met her, she acted out a metaphorical drama reminiscent of this occurrence.

The dad is working hard. He's tired. Mom gets up and she's tired. She stumbles around. The ladies come to visit. The dad was so tired, because he had to sweep every day. The dad put poison in a hole so it made him die. He put poison and a rubber thing on him. Heaven cannot fix him so the dinosaurs eat him. The dad was so tired he had to take a rest. He was so tired. . . .

In another case, my child client played out a more literal story-line about two babies who had died! Her mother had recently spontaneously aborted a baby. However, her daughter did not know anything about the abortion. Even more peculiarly, when I told the mother that I found it rather confusing that her daughter had played that two babies had died, rather than one, her face instantly flushed as her mouth fell open. She immediately disclosed to me that she had actually lost twins—but that no one, other than her doctor and the hospital staff, knew about this.

Can you believe the wisdom of these kids on the sixth branch of the Spiritual Tree of Life? Their brilliance as healers through their play and the use of metaphor forever astounds me. Despite their young ages, they have tremendous potential, never failing to bless us with the bright light of knowing that forever permeates them.

🍃

What to Know, Say, and Do
for Spiritual Partners on the Sixth Branch

Watch for recurrent themes in your children's healing play. The topics will give you hints about their journeys, since their play at home may be healing play as well. Learn about movies and books that would give them places with which to identify and heal. For instance, *Lion King* is suitable for a child who feels responsible for the death of his parent. I have listed other movies appropriate for spiritual children in the resource section in the back of this book.

Spiritual kids do not thrive when conflict between their parents is a part of their daily lives. They would sooner manage the grief of a breakup than being constantly torn between two people they love. Divorce can be a manageable journey of grief; a continuous war, however, leaves a spiritual child feeling hopeless without the power to change things, and it is a difficult situation for children whose unwavering desire is for peace. Clarifying statements may be helpful. "I know it tears you up when your parents fight because your nature is to seek peace. You want to change things, but realize you can do nothing. Sometimes you feel helpless."

If you are a parent experiencing the conflict of separation or divorce, limit your children's exposure to the conflict. When they are aware of the tension between the two of you, let them speak openly about their feelings. Be aware of the intensity of conflict in their play. Listen with a kind and compassionate heart. *Never* argue with them about their thoughts and feelings, especially about the other parent. Simply maintain your spiritual partner role of benevolent guide and teacher, clarifying and communicating love and support.

Participating in their healing play can be extremely advantageous for strengthening your relationship with your children as well as with their spiritual world. Follow their lead. If they resist your involvement in play, wait until you are welcomed. When you begin to participate, however, you will know them even more intimately and will enjoy closeness and sharing you may never have thought possible. Your spiritual partnership may blossom into a healing relationship of unconditional support and honesty.

Be aware that when unusually sensitive spiritual children are traumatized, they are likely to playfully torment their spiritual partners to show them the extent of their distress. If you are presented with this situation and feel you can handle it, set firm limits that are acceptable to you: "If we are to play this way, *no one* is to get hurt. If our play becomes scary or upsetting to either of us, then we will stop immediately." Be sure to set a time limit, and keep some notes regarding the nature of the encounter. If they begin to engage in uncomfortable games or dramas, say, "I am not feeling comfortable with this play. Can we play something else instead?" It's important to communicate acceptance when you set a firm, protective limit.

Boys and girls on the sixth branch brilliantly portray their lives in their playful stories, sometimes metaphorical, sometimes literal. If you are not completely comfortable with the themes you see in your child's play within a few weeks, get help from a therapist or other professional who can be valuable in assisting your children on their spiritual journeys.

Confirm your kids' spiritual needs as they enjoy the amazing benefits of healing play:

- Identify recurrent themes in their healing play.
- Receive with a compassionate ear their feelings of hopelessness.
- Point out similarities on your spiritual journey.

Comfort them:

- Play with them while remaining aware of the intensity of conflict in their play.
- Enhance metaphors by using characters and events that arise naturally in their play.

- Wait for them to welcome you into their play.
- Remember that their play at home may be healing play as well.
- Set firm boundaries, especially when playing with traumatized children.
- Never communicate rejection.
- Contact a therapist or other professional to assist your children when more help is needed.
- If you are a parent experiencing the conflict of separation or divorce, limit your children's exposure to the conflict.

Communicate with them:
- Become aware of movies and books that would give your children places with which to identify (refer to the resource section in the back of this book).
- Read and watch together.
- Encourage them to reach out to persons other than their parents for a continued sense of belonging, especially when faced with family dissolution.
- When your children are aware of the tension between the two of you, let them speak openly about their feelings.

Transformation

7

Spiritual kids embrace the joy and pain of transformation, the seventh branch of the Spiritual Tree of Life. Change not only is second nature to these kids but also a source of enjoyment, creativity, wonder, healing, and celebration. They are fascinated with the metamorphosis of caterpillars into butterflies, for example. They engage in vigorous movement in their healing play: from trauma to triumph, despair to hope, and life to death, always followed by a return to life in some form.

Even though it is natural for them to shed their old lives on the road to spiritual rebirth, when they suffer profound losses and trauma they may find themselves stripped of everything that helped them to feel secure. At those times their journeys may be long and agonizing. They are challenged to revisit parts of themselves and redefine who they are in light of their altered world. On the seventh branch, they often play out themes of death that symbolize the destruction of their lives as they have known them. As on the fifth branch, they frequently encounter evil, creating battles in which they conquer the enemy.

Often having experienced abuse, exploitation, or neglect, these children's recurring themes of being alone and abandoned with nowhere to hide from their distress are coupled with nightmares of mutilation, such as animals or monsters eating them, as well as fears of future losses. Their spiritual and psychological turmoil is intensely colored with the darkness of agonizing grief. Anger, hopelessness, and guilt are predominant feelings they are compelled to communicate, with any luck in the presence of a spiritual partner.

Navigating the waters of transformation is at best a challenge. While many kids say they no longer have a will to live, they find themselves at odds with their surroundings. A war rages within them; they sometimes feel like lost souls hopelessly riding the rough waters of the dark sea for long periods of time. Often evident in them are their two sides—their deeply loving and caring side coupled with their intense anger and fear. Managing the opposing forces thrusts these otherwise peace-loving boys and girls into intense inner conflict that without expression and validation may threaten to destroy them.

To further display their feelings of entrapment, kids on this branch sometimes handcuff or tie their therapist with scarves or ropes and repeatedly "shoot" them. They may also cover their own body parts in the sand, occasionally requesting to be totally immersed except for their heads. All of these activities appear to demonstrate the intense suffering their confinement on this painful journey has caused them.

Having lost nearly all they have known that is safe and comforting, they are on frightening journeys through worlds of darkness. In their play they are assaulted by destructive forces such as tornadoes, ice storms, and hurricanes. At the same time, they are compelled to interact with a variety of threatening figures in addition to the skeleton: monsters, zombies, vampires, ghosts, witches, snakes, robots, and devils. While these figures are reminders of their loss, when in their play they fearlessly overcome them, their healing journeys are usually nearing completion.

These children learn great lessons as they are challenged with massive changes, usually as a result of dreadful life events. Although they may appear ordinary during this inescapably agonizing journey, with adequate support they are transformed into extraordinary people with great resilience and inner resources. Despite their heartache they are honest and courageous, with a spiritual depth, wisdom, and steadfast belief in the goodness of the world.

Usually on this branch, relationships with God or a higher self are intensified. Unseen worlds in which they participate may also strengthen their spiritual lives. Their capacity to connect intimately with others is deepened, which also places them on the second branch of compassion and belonging.

Jeremy

Four-year-old Jeremy spent much of his time on the seventh branch. He persistently alternated between playing with the skeleton, which he described as "the most powerful of the evil ones," and with the policeman who fought the skeleton. One time he said, "Mollie, today I am the skeleton! I will destroy anyone who guards over Jeremy! The policeman will die first!" Another time he exclaimed, "Mollie, now I am the policeman. The skeleton hurt me, but I am still alive! Actually, I am stronger than ever!" Although he often chose to be the policeman, a symbol of protection from evil, he would question his ability to defeat the skeleton. Despite his self-doubts and fears upon which the evil he fought thrived, he never failed to confront the skeleton—the symbol of power and darkness in his play. The war raged within him and without.

On the seventh branch, these kids dismember their dolls, superheroes, and others, sometimes burying them in the sand headfirst. For instance, Jeremy solemnly dismembered the beast toys or the evil ones—as though he believed there was an established procedure. His play appeared ceremonial, similar to a priest visiting the sick or burying the dead. He said, "There, Mollie, this beast lost his arm and this one his leg. Now what is this one going to lose? Mollie, help me do this! See, some of the beasts have lost their arms and legs! They cannot breathe under the sand!"

Michael and Ashley

Michael's grandmother brought Michael, a wonderfully alive and emotionally vulnerable spiritual kid, to me to help him deal with the aftermath of his parents' divorce. Although they were cousins, Michael and Ashley referred to each other as brother and sister. They spent their first few years in their grandparents' household: Ashley with her mother and Michael with both his parents. However, Michael's relationship to his grandmother was more like a son to a mother, and his deep spiritual connection to Ashley transcended all time and space.

Michael was a child who did not feel safe. He had a repeated dream that he was falling off his bed and dogs were eating him. He looked for mean people in the playroom, shooting them, "until they are all dead." He bragged as he killed the plastic snakes, "I'm a good killer for those snakes. I'm the best snake killer in the world. I'm strong and brave like Hercules!" He seemed to realize that his life would require great inner strength.

Michael described being sexually abused by several people, particularly his father. Although his story and play were convincing, the authorities were never willing to make a determination of guilt. His parents ended his therapy about six weeks after I confronted them and reported their son's statements to Social Services. Despite all the pressure on him, Michael never changed the basic content of his story, consistently disclosing to his next therapist many of the events he had described to his grandmother and me.

He blossomed during the few weeks when he was allowed only supervised time with his father. Playing out his exploitation over and over again with concentrated energy, he focused on gaining power and ridding his world of abuse. In his innocence he told me with great hope and excitement, "I told the truth and now the social-worker woman is going to make my dad stay away from me. And I'm glad. It's all because of those bad things he did to me!" Now that he had told the truth—exposed his horrible secret—he believed he would be safe.

Unfortunately, Michael was not protected for long. He was returned to the custody of his parents and soon moved out of state, further isolating him from Ashley, his grandparents, and all the other family members who were so important to him.

Ashley began to have nightmares, crying out in fear to her mother and grandmother. She was now six years old; she was four when Michael had moved away.

Ashley had no guarantee that Michael was in a safe place. She said to her grandmother, "Let's go save Michael!" Anytime she made a wish or said a prayer, she would look earnestly to the heavens and say, "Please bring Michael back to me! He is my brother!" With compassion she told her mother, "Michael is in trouble! I know he is not safe! We must help him!"

Ghosts, skeletons, and monsters haunted Ashley both in her play and elsewhere. In the playroom, when she heard a noise she would say anxiously,

I think that is a ghost! I know there is a ghost haunting our house. The ghost comes at nighttime, when we all go to bed. If the mommies don't go to sleep, they will turn into spirits. The mommies and that mean old cranky boy are going to be mean ghosts. My mother and grandmother are dying. All of my family has turned into spirits, first of all, then ghosts, then skeletons. Where's the ghost, Mollie? Where's the skeleton?

On her spiritual journey, Ashley was symbolically reduced to a skeleton of the person she had been as she grieved the loss of her cousin and fearfully anticipated losing her mother and grandmother. She frequently told me, "Last night I had a nightmare that Mommy and Grandma took me to a fun park. When we were there, two robber guys stole me and they put me in a closet. They taped my mouth and tied my hands and feet." Over and over she played that she was shooting and killing the bad guys. Her nightmares, as intense as they were, metaphorically portrayed the terrifying insecurity she felt about her safety and Michael's.

Ashley's play was full of frightening events such as "scary picnics" with zombies that attacked her. For several months Ashley, like Michael, would insist that I go with her on the same scary picnic that Michael, unbeknownst to Ashley, had described in his play. She would select the creepiest, meanest, and most powerful puppets for those sessions. She went back and forth between being the victim and the one who had hurt both Michael and herself.

As Ashley completed her fear-provoking journey, she built her life on a strong spiritual foundation. Using her creative resources, she befriended Froggie, the cuddly, huge green frog puppet who was a sweet-natured and protective spiritual partner for her. She called him her brother, insisting that she have him near her at all times, especially during the scary picnics that were becoming less frightening. As her battle became less intense, she revealed that Froggie had saved her life many times. At the end of her journey of transformation, she found Froggie to be her place of peace as well as an inseparable buddy.

Luke

Luke was lovingly accompanied by his parents, a younger brother, and a younger sister who was developmentally disabled from birth. Luke's family, especially sister Beth, undoubtedly played with him on the seventh branch.

Never have I met a boy who loved his family more intensely; never have I met a child who absorbed his family's pain more than Luke. He was an amazingly spiritual child whose suffering greatly intensified when he found himself trapped in a vicious cycle of love and caring accompanied by the anger, guilt, and hopelessness expressed from his grief.

Luke believed he had lost his family when his sister was born. She never became more than a baby, and it was not possible for his parents to attend to Luke and his brother with the same vitality they gave Beth. Despite their extraordinary love for him, Luke felt alone and abandoned, as though his parents no longer cared about him. When I met him at age seven, his anger was unmanageable. His parents were deeply concerned.

Luke's spiritual wisdom was shaped by teachings from his Christian upbringing, his parents' reinforcement of these beliefs, and his basic sensitive and caring nature. Thus, when he felt such intense anger toward the family he dearly treasured, he believed he was a bad person. The more he told himself, "You cannot feel this way!" the angrier he became. As he secretly wished that bad things would happen to his helpless sister and he occasionally physically attacked his parents, he began to live with a deep sense of guilt. In an attempt to show how trapped he felt, he often handcuffed me while shooting me repeatedly. One time he told me without hesitation, "Beth takes away most of the attention. I am kind of lonely, but mostly mad at my family."

Luke's mother told me that Luke was in many ways "a perfect child who moved from model behavior to explosive episodes of great proportion."

Luke gets angry and lashes out, mostly at me, about every three or four weeks. In his latest episode he broke his brother's play mobile toy as he went into a tizzy. Luke then went into the living room and started pounding on pillows. He hit me. I just ignored him, but he escalated until he lost the privilege of his favorite riding lessons. Then he stood on the stairs yelling at the top of his lungs that he would rather lose anything other than his riding lessons. It took him half an hour to calm down.

As is common in many kids on the seventh branch, the fantasies that Luke played out suggested both a strong caring quality as well as an intense resentment concerning Beth's overwhelming intrusiveness into his life. Lovingly, he expressed his desire that she no longer suffer as he played that he was a physician who diagnosed, healed, and kept her from death. In the dollhouse he made a little girl figurine do all the things Beth could not do. Each week he carefully put her to bed and closed the dollhouse as though to tuck her in safely. He then moved to the sand table, where he enacted a war in which all the bad guys were killed.

Luke would cry out in his play as a way of reminding both himself and his family of what they had lost. He repeated with a chantlike quality, "Remember, this is a happy house!" With puppets Luke orchestrated the following drama about Frankie, a boy much like himself whose life is shattered.

The tank comes along and blows Frankie away. Frankie is one of two sons who live with their farmer dad, mother, and dog. Frankie becomes a raccoon robot for Halloween. Then all bad things start to happen to him. The boy thinks that he lives in a happy house, but he discovers that he lives in a haunted house. The happy house he used to know became a scary spooky house. He says, "I am lucky that more bad things did not happen. They would have happened if the spook had not come and the boy had not flown back in the house."

As much as Luke considered Beth's presence to have created "bad things" for him, he appreciated her plight. He expressed the anger and hurt he believes she suffered.

The family is going to bed in their clothes because they are too tired to put on pajamas. The next morning the little girl wakes her parents up by knocking them out of bed. The little girl pushes her parents and the maids down two flights of stairs. They are hurt, but there are no broken bones. They have oatmeal and hot tea for breakfast. The little girl says, "I'm lonely. I'd like some friends to play with. I am mad at the maid, so I will leave all the beds unmade and the breakfast table all a mess."

While faced with massive losses on every front, Luke portrayed his inner conflict by eventually finding a peaceful resolution.

The two captains unexpectedly yelled, "Stop fighting!" They both came out and made peace. Then both sides went back to their camps. Suddenly magic came to the battlefield and the dead people rose up. One good guy hung around to be sure no more fighting started. He cleared the battlefield with a tractor. He told the soldiers at the White House that the war was over and the little girl was safe and sound. And they never had a war again!

Beth died when she was almost eleven years old. Luke's love, along with the immense support of his family, sustained Beth to live almost nine years longer than expected. Within the context of her role as sister, daughter, and much-cherished member of her community, her life took on great purpose. Luke described her presence as teaching others how to reach out and love as well as how to be loved. He believed that his sister, like himself, his brother, and even his parents, was a spiritual child.

Brooke

Brooke felt so miserably responsible for the emotional and physical well-being of her family, especially her physically handicapped brother, that she believed she would not be able to live. Instinctively, she went on a journey of deep spiritual transformation that was healing to her soul, awakening in her an acceptance of the instability of life. She described this pilgrimage in great detail—and with mixed emotions of happiness, fear, and confusion.

I was reading in the bathtub the other day, when I realized how easily I could die. I thought I was going to die soon. I started to imagine all the deaths I could think of—like Grandma, Princess Diana, and the guys on the mountain. I must have dozed off, because I had this dream. The last thing I remembered was dropping my book. Then in my dream I went under the water, blowing out air. Then I sort of died. Everything went black and I was floating through a tunnel. I saw a mural of the Last Supper, the one made by Michelangelo. Jesus was in the background. There was a woman wrapped up in white with long blonde hair that was sort of wavy.

As I went flying through the tunnel, the one life verse that kept me going, "Do not be afraid, for I am with you," was written on the wall with a light above it. Next to the words was a picture of Jesus' hand touching someone. I was floating. I looked straight ahead and I saw a big light in a triangular form. I swam up the tunnel toward the light. Strange women were singing. I couldn't see them. I just heard them. I went into the light and the tunnel behind me closed. It was all steamy. There was a big fridge and in it I found tons of half-and-half bottles. I love half-and-half!

Nobody asked me anything. I just started talking out loud. It was like God was asking me why I should go to heaven— why he should let me in heaven. He didn't really say it, but I knew he was asking me, so I said, "Because I love you, and I have given you my heart." I waited a little bit and nothing happened. I had a pretty purple dress on and a crown. Then the gates opened up, and I went through them before they shut. Inside I saw all my relatives, and ancestors, and Grandma. They had a party for me, and they showed me my house. I could drink half-and-half all the time. A new one always appeared when I finished the old one.

Brooke said that as quickly as she had left, she was back at home in the bathtub under water blowing out air. She had completely lost track of time. The whole experience actually took only a few seconds, but it seemed like an eternity. Brooke told her parents not to be sad when she dies, because she'll be in heaven waiting for them. She no longer feared death, nor was she obsessed with imagining many different ways of dying. She no longer believed that she would die soon. She was greatly strengthened as she began to reach out for life with a deepened sense of the richness of her spiritual resources.

When children successfully complete this challenging and often excruciating step toward healing themselves and their world, they gain a stronger, more authentic sense of self. In the process they experience movement from agonizing loss to an unyielding reclamation of life. At the end of the journey they find inner peace as they build their lives on strong spiritual foundations with all the richness of their never-ending resources. While embarking on their new lives with strength and vitality, they realize the joy of virtual rebirth.

What to Know, Say, and Do
for Spiritual Partners on the Seventh Branch

Spiritual children often blame themselves, have poor self-esteem, and are irritable and angry when they suffer great losses. Stay in close communication with them. With your love and support, help them to validate their journeys while creatively bringing them to life. Writing letters to ones they have lost may be a helpful tool.

They sometimes have dreams or nightmares that are metaphors of their journeys. Ask them to tell you their dreams and suggest that they draw pictures of them, sometimes making small illustrated books. If you have similar dreams, which often is true of parents and their spiritual children, share them. If not, establish a common ground by telling them stories about distressful times in your life and how you survived and were enriched by them, while always validating the difficult nature of their struggles. As spiritual partners, respond to their stories by enthusiastically supporting their wisdom and courage as spiritual children. Your supportive comments may be something like, "Tell us more! There was a tunnel? What did it look like? You had a meaningful godlike journey. Let's celebrate! This is so wonderful!"

Help your spiritual children understand their sensitive natures as well as the journeys on which they have embarked. Encouraging and validating these kids is crucial to their development and adjustment.

Offer support by making it clear why being on the seventh branch causes so much distress: "You have a big heart. It is easy for you to love people. It is hard on you when you don't want to be close to someone." Their response may be, "I didn't know you knew how sad and angry I've been about my family!" Then they are no longer alone in their sorrow. Point out that feelings of anger are normal, especially while suffering such tremendous losses. Validate them for their courage in honestly expressing their anger with you. Create awareness through metaphor that they are shedding their old lives on the road to spiritual rebirth. They can then look forward to positive end results.

Your children's family situations may require additional spiritual partners, friends, and extended family that consistently spend quality time to help them renew their belief in the goodness of life. Family meetings in which all members participate to share feelings and solve problems are also valuable for spiritual kids who are feeling disconnection in their lives.

Spiritual children who have successfully journeyed through the "dark night of the soul" are likely to be awakened and sensitized to the pain of others and have an exaggerated desire for connection with them. They are dependent on you to create opportunities for such closeness and support.

Children on the seventh branch are meeting a formidable challenge. If they continue to appear troubled after a few weeks, consult a therapist who will have insights and compassion for their courageous journeys.

Confirm your kids' spiritual needs as they are met with the challenges of transformation:
- Empathize with them about the losses they have suffered.
- Help them to understand that loss and trauma can lead to many challenges.
- Treat irritability, anger, and poor self-esteem as signs of depression, often from loss.
- Validate their unique needs, feelings, and experiences.

Comfort them:
- Be there for them no matter how tough times get.
- Make them aware that, despite hard times, their path will lead them to freedom and joy.
- Offer additional spiritual partners for support, such as spiritually aware professional counselors or others involved in enrichment programs.
- Recall stories of fun times.
- Create opportunities for closeness.

Communicate with them:
- Explain to them your understanding of their distressful journeys.
- Ask them about dreams and nightmares.
- Suggest they draw pictures or make books about their journeys.
- Discuss the concepts of death and loss.
- Show interest in their stories of dreams and daytime imaginings about death and transformation.

Afterword

Spiritual Partners in Today's World

Spiritual children everywhere are crying out for support on their unique journeys. They need spiritual partners who are invested in their safety and well-being while listening with a compassionate ear and communicating interest, acceptance, comfort, and kinship. Such partners are companions who encourage, protect, acknowledge, and appreciate their children's innate spiritual nature. And while they share stories and information with their spiritual boys and girls, these adults are likely to benefit by allowing their own spirituality to blossom again. Thus, spiritual partnership is a reciprocal road between adults and kids, with each igniting a flame within the other.

Spiritual partners don't have to go it alone. There are many supportive resources in the form of movies, books, and websites, some of which are listed in the resource section of this book. In addition, they may find support groups by going online.

Rejection

Despite their desire to find spiritual partners, spiritual children often meet a world that rejects who they are and what they experience.

This rejection may be as subtle as not recognizing the importance of recurring dreams or as blatant as adults who criticize with such statements as "What's wrong with you? There is no such thing as an imaginary friend," "You really shouldn't feel that way," or "You don't feel that way!" Thus, seeing themselves as outcasts, these kids begin to suffer the destructive effects of isolation born of their spiritual giftedness.

Often, parents of the children in my playroom knew of the hurtful circumstances in their children's lives. However, most of those children never felt it was safe to disclose to anyone, including their parents, the spiritual aspects of their stories, which the kids considered to be unusual or even forbidden. When I questioned them, many responded, "Are you kidding? I would never tell my parents about that! They don't believe me." Indeed, most parents who were aware of their children's spiritual gifts were critical and protective, fearful that others learning of the experiences would judge and perhaps shun their children as well as themselves.

Spiritual kids benefit from an expanded consciousness that, in its basic form, is like a seed waiting to be planted in good ground, watered, and fertilized. Depending on the amount of nutrients and attention it receives, the seed may sprout and begin to form as the plant it was intended to be. It may thrive and make new leaves each day; eventually, with enough care it may create its flowers and fruit. On the other hand, the seed may develop into a plant that lives a long and fruitless life, maintaining the few leaves it initially developed while dropping flower buds. From the same seed of consciousness, a plant may be created that never has the strength to move toward the sun. The ground around it hardens so the plant cannot accept nourishment. Before long it withers and dies.

To many adults, a spiritual child's world is threatening, on some level reminding them of their own painful loss of innocence, intuition, sensitivity, and connection to their global family. Despite their sincere wish to be helpful, it is difficult for those adults to guide their children with insight and compassion. They have shut out their capacity to be healing toward themselves, their families, and their communities. Thus, one generation cripples the next until our young spiritual people are further and further from realizing their potential. At risk for losing their precious gifts, they ultimately become members in the conspiracy to cripple yet another generation.

As parents join their kids on the Spiritual Tree of Life, sometimes they do remember their earlier, spiritual lives. For instance, an eight-year-old girl on the fourth branch told her mother about her guardian angel; consequently, her mother relived her experience with the spiritual guardian of her childhood. Another child on the fourth branch described the lights she sees around people; her father remembered that he had seen rainbows around friends and family when he was a boy. Connecting through a common base of experience offers invaluable support and validation to kids who might otherwise feel weird and alone.

Relationship

To gain children's trust, spiritual partners must walk a sometimes rocky road hand-in-hand with them. As this relationship blossoms into a safe place of self-disclosing, true belonging, and connection, they will enjoy one another's worlds, both seen and unseen. For instance, the partners will not merely acknowledge their children's companions but will welcome and even help celebrate their special presence. In this encouraging environment, boys and girls will be free to openly disclose stories of their spiritual experiences.

While building trusting relationships, spiritual partners emphasize imagination and creativity rather than the importance of reality. They appreciate that *real* and *imaginary* are close relatives, with *real* no longer occupying a more valid place of truth over that which is based on imagination. The invalidating statement "Oh, that was *only* your imagination!" is no longer applicable.

Spiritual children have a natural inclination to express themselves creatively. A six-year-old girl shared that she had been in trouble many times for her imagination.

I know that imagination is the most important thing in the whole world. After I got in trouble a few times—I remember those bad days—I decided for a while that I would never use my imagination again. I was two then. After a couple of years I changed my mind. I decided to use my imagination, even if it meant that I would get in trouble. Imagination is very important!

A seven-year-old boy shared what he referred to as his invisible world by introducing me to all its participants through the playroom puppets. He called it Bryan's Animal World because many of the characters were animals. If I referred to the world that is separate from his animal world as the "real world," he expressed his objections to this, saying that each world is as real as the other.

Bryan's mother was an intimate part of Bryan's Animal World. She was protective and reassuring; in no way did she make demands for him to change anything about his story. I became a welcomed visitor into his world by believing everything he told me, thereby giving him a means to safely and creatively express who he is. His trust in me developed more easily as a result of the nurturing relationship he enjoyed with his mother, who was clearly his primary spiritual partner.

It is important for spiritual partners to frequently and openly praise their children, never appearing to be ashamed of them. For instance, Kyle's mother speaks proudly of her son's spiritual prowess by telling the recent story of their family getting caught in a blinding Montana spring blizzard while driving on the highway. With great enthusiasm in earshot of six-year-old Kyle, she described the scary situation that worsened within a few hours. Just at the moment that she was considering pulling off the road, Kyle volunteered, "Mom, remember how Dad said to pray if the weather gets too bad. Well, I think it's time now that I say some prayers." He became very quiet for a few minutes with his eyes shut tightly.

Within minutes of his prayer, an Indian family drove up alongside them and spoke to Kyle's mother, offering her their home as a place to stay or, if they wished, guidance to a motel for the night. They safely followed the welcome strangers to a nearby motel that they never could have found in the whiteout conditions of the storm. Upon hearing his mother's story, Kyle smiled contentedly and merely commented on never having seen so much snow!

Spiritual partners must encourage their boys and girls when they describe having had mystical experiences such as contact with angels, fairies, and deceased relatives; seeing auras; and having near-death experiences. For instance, if you are aware that your children have spiritual companions, show interest by asking for updates: "How is your angel? Have any of your spiritual companions visited you lately?"

Your involvement may become even more crucial if your children are afraid of their spirits. When eight-year-old Caleb became increasingly fearful of his spirits, his mother helped him by accepting and protecting him and by encouraging him to protect himself.

Sometimes it's just like they are flashing. I'll see a spirit really fast. Then when I look away and back, it will be gone. They have different shapes of animals—the head of a snake and the back of a dog. One spirit comes and goes, comes and goes. Sometimes he's scary. My mom told me to tell him to go away when he's scary. He usually listens to me.

Caleb had not realized how powerful he could be over his visitors. With the help of his mother as a spiritual partner, he was not alone on his journey.

While offering boys and girls support, confidence, and a sense of self-worth, spiritual partners teach them how to use their gifts responsibly. At the same time, spiritual kids need to enjoy a healthy emotional life supported by the awareness that feelings are not good or bad; it is the resultant behaviors that need to be addressed. Their mistakes are forgiven; they are not judged or criticized but are encouraged to continue to explore their spirituality.

Boys and girls who have not actualized their hidden potential to be spiritual children may greatly profit from being told stories of other children's experiences. These narratives may lay the ground-work for otherwise spiritually inhibited children to understand the incredible possibilities within their reach.

A Test of Trust

When children begin sharing their spiritual world, a testing ground may develop. If adults can be trusted, honest and dynamic relation-ships will begin to develop. If they communicate lack of support or rejection, however, children will hide (become "invisible") as they learn to present suitable façades, ultimately shutting the door to their private space and keeping out potential spiritual partners whom they now consider intruders.

Therefore, based on trusting or destructive relationships, chil-dren will make up their minds whether or not they can trust them-selves or other adults. They will decide it is either OK to be themselves or that something is wrong with them and begin to shut down their awareness. If the latter, they will consider their gifts and wisdom unfortunate baggage as well as sources of fear and poor self-esteem, precursors to a lifetime of pain and struggle. They will have lost their most precious possession: their spiritual selves.

It is the responsibility of a child's spiritual partner to uncondi-tionally accept and comfort the child while establishing a sense of spiritual safety, trust, and freedom. Typically, children gain this kind of support only if they communicate feelings and events to their parents, teachers, or caretakers that are acceptable to these adults. Even children's therapists often lack the appropriate openness and insight needed to be a part of the child's world. According to Melvin Morse's *Closer to the Light*, a good example of this extreme closedness on the part of a psychologist is the story of a five-year-old boy who had a near-death experience.

His experience transformed him to the extent that even in grade school he often told the other children of the importance to love one another. If questioned, he would share with his classmates and teachers his experience of seeing God. Morse says, "This led to problems in class, and eventually, he was sent to school psychologists, who told him that he had too vivid an imagination."[3] This experience unnecessarily led to years of intense loneliness, poor self-esteem, and suffering on the part of the boy.

This child desperately needed validation and support regarding his powerfully meaningful life-changing experience. Instead he was branded as a boy who was merely making up stories from his imagination. Since the psychologist who made this statement was a person with much perceived power, the boy and his parents feared that there was something wrong with him, perhaps that he was crazy. Not only was the boy destructively labeled, he was not given the appropriate recognition and comfort that he needed to freely understand and accept his own experience. As a result of the therapist's criticism, the boy questioned his own personal integrity and imagination, gifts basic to his spiritual personhood and healing.

These children enter adolescence with the quality of their lives subtly and gradually diminished. Without the support of spiritual partners, they are often confused, distrustful, withdrawn, and angry. They usually do not show consideration for the grown-ups in their lives. Because those adults had shown the children no respect, the children now reciprocate. They demonstrate these feelings with an intensity of anger or depression that is in relation to the intensity of abuse or neglect they have known. That anger is the last remnant of their aliveness and evidence of their vague sense of loss, which is difficult for them to define and articulate.

Adolescents who have already constructed walls to isolate themselves from the loss of their childhood truths reinforce the walls between their elders and themselves. Many become permanently entrapped within their own fortresses of pain and denial. Rather than looking within themselves as gifted spiritual beings to find something beautiful to explore, adolescents often look to their peers for acceptance and recognition of self. They demonstrate their awareness of how deadly conformity is by developing subcultures in which they dress, talk, think, and act differently from the established mores. Yet for the most part, they are hungering for the support of spiritual partners.

The people with whom they choose to spend their lives, the decisions they make about jobs, and the ways in which they entertain themselves all become random determinations based on accident, availability, or boredom. The convenience of alcohol and drugs may numb their pain. They are no longer on the path of self-awareness, truth, and growth. Rather than suffer with the pain of being a lost and lonely reject, they let others define who they are, which further alienates them from their innate wisdom.

Recently, a depressed fifteen-year-old came into my playroom for the first time. She was a beautiful young woman stylishly dressed. She did not allow eye contact, and her face was frozen in an expression of sadness. Her somewhat tough exterior was not congruent with the fact that in the waiting room she had volunteered to read a book to a child she did not know.

The girl's father had recently killed himself. Although she was experiencing a great deal of turmoil while grieving him, she found it very difficult to share her life and feelings with anyone, especially those outside the family. Slowly and painfully, with a great deal of encouragement and self-disclosure on my part, she began to describe her journey. At one point the tears welled up. Rather than commenting on the death of her father, she said, while looking around the playroom at all the toys, "I am really sad that I cannot be a child any longer. It's so hard for me to put it into words, but I don't like being all grown up. I just want to be a kid again."

Adolescents are not usually clear why they are angry and depressed, except that they feel that something is not right, that somehow they have been "ripped off." Inevitably, as these young people enter adulthood, the loss of self gains momentum. As adults they may realize many successes yet still experience an underlying, pervasive sense of sadness. On the surface it appears that these mature individuals have everything needed for happiness. At the same time they often lead miserable lives, having lost touch with their spiritual giftedness.

Recovery

But a return to the truth, recovery of wholeness, and reclamation of a quality way of life are still possible. In *Psychological Reflections*, Carl Jung offers hope:

> An archetype is like an old watercourse along which the water of life has flowed for centuries, digging a deep channel for itself. The longer it has flowed in this channel the more likely it is that sooner or later the water will return to its old bed.[4]

My hope is that you, as spiritual partners, will validate your children's remarkable wisdom and compassion while embracing their experiences, feelings, thoughts, and beliefs. And I challenge you to continue to open your own spiritual doors to new awareness as you reconnect with your spiritual child within and share in the happiness and struggle your boys and girls experience. In your mutual search for the truth, you can support your kids by recognizing that together you are a source of strength and comfort for one another. Finally, may you and your kids peacefully unite as part of a world community and understand the power, beauty, and brilliance of spiritual partnership in today's world.

www.childrensspiritualintelligence.com

Questionnaire
An Enhancement Tool for Communication

Who are spiritual children? What makes them tick? When did they begin their unique journeys? What do they need from their spiritual partners? Are they driven to heal the wounds of the world? Are they really peacemakers at heart?

Communication between spiritual partners and children is crucial. However, many parents and even healthcare professionals are not aware of the appropriate questions they need to ask to explore spiritual children's characteristics and interests. Answering the following questions will help your spiritual children and you as their partners to assess and encourage their journeys. Remember to make your dialoguing fun and intimate, and always be open and accepting of your children's responses. Explore answers to these questions in relation to your own life as well.

1. *Is it important to love one another?* How do you show your love?

2. *What are your ideas about war?* Do you think it is necessary? Would you want to fight a war with a country where your friends live?

3. *How are you different from people in other countries, other churches, other schools?* How are you the same? What do you like/dislike about the differences you see? Is it OK to be different?

4. *Who are your best friends?* Why? Are they like you in most ways, or are you very different from one another?

5. *Do you think of people in other countries as your brothers and sisters?* Do you hurt when they are suffering, such as from an earthquake or otherwise? Are you a sponge that soaks up other people's misery?

6. *In what country did your ancestors live?* Have you ever been there, or to any foreign country? Do you speak any languages other than English? Do you want to learn?

7. *Describe your dream trip around the world.* Would you like to meet children from other countries? If you did, what would you do together? What questions might you ask each other? How would you stay in touch with your new friends? Do you have a pen pal in another country?

8. *Have you ever spoken with God or another spiritual being?* Where were you? What did you learn from your conversation?

9. *Do you ever play that there is a war between the good guys and the bad guys?* Do you sometimes play you are fighting against ghosts, skeletons, or other scary monsters? How do you feel after you play out this war?

10. *Do you have the same dream over and over again?* Do you pretend these dreams are real in your play? Have you told anyone about your dreams and play?

11. *Do you feel bad inside when another kid is mean, a bully picks on you, you fight with your brothers and sisters, or your parents have a fight?*

12. *Is telling the truth important to you?*

13. *Do you have a special job to do while on earth?* For instance, are you a teacher, healer, or peacemaker?

14. *How did you feel when the World Trade Center towers were destroyed?*

15. *Have your parents been through a divorce, or have you known a kid whose parents were getting a divorce?* How do you feel about this?

16. *Do you have experiences you keep a secret?* Would you be rejected if others knew about your secrets? Who do you trust?

17. *Have you, or are you presently, going through a tough time?* Is there someone who understands you and can help you through this hard time?

18. *Do you have an angel or maybe several?* What can you tell about them?

19. *Do you have other imaginary or spiritual companions?* Who are they? What do they look like? Are they nice? Do they scare you? Do they help you in some way? Can you tell anyone about them?

20. *Do you know people who have died?* Do you ever see them or visit with them? Have they become your guardian angels? Do they help you with your life? What do they say to you? Can you tell anyone about them? Do you feel afraid, weird, or lonely because you have visitors who are invisible to others?

21. *What is death?* When people die, do they go away forever?

22. *Do you have a special house, cabin, castle, or other safe place you often visit in your imagination or dreams?* What is it like? Would you ever invite someone else to go with you?

23. *Do you have dreams about flying?* Do you remember when you could fly? If so, is it important for you to fly again? Have you ever told anyone about this?

24. *Do you ever travel in your spirit to other worlds that may be invisible to adults?*

25. *Do you have a vivid imagination?* Can you tell others about your imagination? Do you like to play imaginary games? Are you ever rejected because of your creativity and imagination?

26. *Do you ever see rainbows, lights, or colors around people?* Can you tell anyone about this wonderful gift?

27. *Do you sometimes have dreams about things that happen later?*

28. *Do you ever just know without anyone telling you that something is going to happen and then it does?*

29. *Would you like to celebrate special days, such as your spiritual companions' birthdays?*

30. *What is something else that is interesting about you?*

Self-Quiz
Are You a Wise and Compassionate Spiritual Partner?

As an adult, do you encourage your child's spiritual intelligence? Answer each statement according to your experiences, beliefs, or feelings. Answer true if it is usually or always true for you. Answer false if it is not very true or not true at all for you. (*SC* refers to spiritual children.)

1. I validate the feelings and experiences of the SC in my life.

2. I do not ever criticize SC's imaginary or spiritual companions.

3. It is essential that I establish a safe and trusting relationship with my SC.

4. I would never make a statement like, "What's wrong with you? There's no such thing as an imaginary companion!"

5. It would be destructive to say to my SC, "You don't feel that way" or "You really shouldn't feel that way."

6. My SC's truths may be different from mine, but I support those truths anyway.

7. SC are gifted human beings.

8. I am not afraid for others to know about the SC in my life.

9. I am not threatened by the beliefs, feelings, or experiences of my SC.

10. I understand the importance to my SC of unconditional acceptance of who they are, how they feel, what they think, where they have been, how they got there, and where they are going.

11. I want my SC to retain their spiritual gifts into adulthood.

12. SC's gifts are invaluable resources for their lives.

13. SC are compassionate healers of themselves, their families, their communities, and the world.

14. SC have a drive to awaken unresolved grief in others.

15. I am available at the drop of a hat to communicate with and empathically support my SC.

16. I honestly share personal stories and insights about my spiritual experiences with my SC.

17. I am open to being vulnerable both by learning from my SC and by teaching others the insights I have gained.

18. I guide my SC without interfering, controlling, or possessing them.

19. I can identify and celebrate my SC's milestones.

20. I know I may not have all the answers, and I can admit this to my inquisitive SC.

21. My SC's self-esteem may be compromised if I do not both appreciate and help them find the meaning, purpose, intent, and use of their gifts as they journey through life.

22. Becoming a spiritual partner is the work of a lifetime.

23. Becoming a spiritual partner cannot be accomplished in isolation.

24. A spiritual partner needs the support of peers, significant others, mentors, and support groups, not unlike my SC's needs.

25. It is crucial that I learn to trust and respect my own unique experiences, feelings, and personhood.

26. It is important that I help my SC to understand their role as peacemaker—that they cannot feel their best in a conflicted or hateful environment.

27. My SC's imagination needs to be unconditionally encouraged, nurtured, and supported.

28. It is important that I help my SC to feel safe and free.

29. I need to guide my SC to be independent, autonomous, self-reliant, and confident so they can grow to make many of their own decisions.

30. I understand the deadliness of judging or criticizing my SC's gifts.

31. I value free time for my SC to play, think, and daydream.

32. If I am a spiritual partner who is also a parent, it is important that my SC and I often have fun, relaxing, intimate times together.

33. I encourage SC to ask questions while exploring any reality.

34. I refuse to engage in a power struggle with my SC.

35. I will guide my SC to respect who they are in truth so they do not become dependent on others' definitions of who they are.

36. SC have deep wisdom and understanding beyond their years.

37. I am willing to encourage SC to bring their world to life with drawings, metaphorical stories, and dramatic play with puppets and other toys.

38. I promote membership in organizations that will enhance my SC's sense of belonging to a community.

39. My role as a spiritual partner is to be an anchor to my SC, helping them remain firmly planted in our reality while journeying to other worlds.

40. Sometimes the journeys of SC and their spiritual partners are similar.

41. SC can benefit from coming in contact with other SC who have had similar experiences.

42. I am open to discuss death with my SC.

43. SC are prone to feel overly responsible and an inordinate amount of shame for unfortunate events in their lives.

44. I support SC in their belief that deceased persons they love still watch over and care about them.

45. SC who have lost a parent to death or through divorce often become obsessed with the fearful notion that they will be left without support as a spiritually gifted individual.

46. SC's sensitivity to the pain in the world sometimes produces anxiety, stress, and guilt.

47. A child who has had a near-death experience may be afraid to speak freely about it.

48. SC teach us that death is always followed by rebirth—a transition from a physically embodied life to one in the spirit.

49. SC are often sensitive to the notion of darkness, which they sometimes battle in their play as they act as spiritual warriors.

50. If my SC have significant spiritual companions whom they describe as evil, it is crucial I seek professional help from a spiritually aware therapist.

All the above are true. To be a wise and compassionate spiritual partner, answering "true" to the greater majority of these statements is desirable.

Keep in mind that, for all of us, becoming a helpful spiritual partner is the work of a lifetime!

Notes

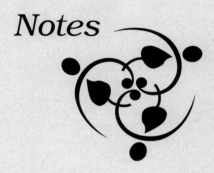

1. John F. Connolly, "Adults Who Had Imaginary Playmates as Children," in *Mental Imagery*, edited by Robert G. Kunzendorf (New York: Plenum Press, 1991). ISBN: 0-306-43825-9

2. Benjamin Hoff, *The Te of Piglet* (New York: Penguin Books USA, 1992). ISBN: 0-14-023016-5

3. Melvin Morse and Paul Perry, *Closer to the Light: Learning from the Near-Death Experiences of Children* (New York: Random House, Villard Books, 1990). ISBN: 0-8041-0832-3

4. Jolande Jacobi and R.F.C. Hull, eds., *C. G. Jung: Psychological Reflections* (Princeton, N.J.: Princeton University Press, 1970). ISBN: 0-691-09862-X

Resources

First Branch: Wisdom and Intuition

Movies

Whale Rider. In this mystical tale, a young Maori girl in New Zealand inspires her family and community to appreciate the power of women.

Simon Birch. This comedy-drama, featuring a narration by Jim Carrey, stars eleven-year-old Ian Michael Smith, who is afflicted with Morquio's syndrome, a genetic disorder that causes dwarfism.

Phenomenon. John Travolta stars as George Malley, who, after being made unconscious by a bright light in the sky, develops amazing intellectual powers.

Books

The Wise Child: A Spiritual Guide to Nurturing Your Child's Intuition, by Sonia Choquette, Ph.D. (New York: Three Rivers Press, 1999). Sonia Choquette is an internationally acclaimed spiritual teacher who has taught many individuals to identify, enhance, and understand their intuitive and creative potential.

Nurturing Spirituality in Children: Simple Hands-On Activities, by Peggy J. Jenkins (Hillsboro, Ore.: Beyond Words Publishing, 1995). This much-needed book offers a variety of heart and spirit lessons that parents can use to instruct their children in less than ten minutes at a time.

Don't Kiss Them Good-bye, by Allison DuBois (New York: Simon and Schuster, Fireside, 2005). Ms. DuBois writes an intriguing true story of her life as a medium, upon which the hit NBC television series is based.

Before I Got Here, edited by Blair Underwood (New York: Atria Books, 2005). Full of wonderful quotes from children, this book shows the inherent wisdom that boys and girls enjoy as they astound us and alter our lives.

Spiritual Intelligence: What We Can Learn from the Early Awakening Child, by Marsha Sinetar (New York: Orbis, 2000). This book inspires us to get in touch with the same gifts that we once enjoyed and spiritually aware children embrace.

The Intuitive Heart, by Henry Reed, Ph. D., and Brenda English (Virginia Beach, Va.: A.R.E. Press, 2000). Henry Reed, a psychologist and expert on human consciousness, endeavors to answer the important questions about whether intuition is real, where it comes from, and how we can learn to use and trust it in our own lives.

Children's Past Lives: How Past Life Memories Affect Your Child, by Carol Bowman (New York: Bantam Books, 1997). Bowman discloses overpowering evidence of children's past-life memories. These accounts are not as uncommon as one might expect.

Other Lives, Other Selves: A Jungian Psychotherapist Discovers Past Lives, by Roger J. Woolger, Ph.D. (New York: Bantam Books, 1988). Enlightening others with an exciting psychotherapeutic approach that results in amazingly helpful emotional and physical outcomes, Dr. Woolger shows how patients unlock the mystery of their deepest memories.

The Survival Guide for Parents of Gifted Kids: How to Understand, Live With, and Stick Up for Your Gifted Child, by Sally Yahnke Walker and Susan K. Perry (Minneapolis, Minn.: Free Spirit Publishing, 1991). This resource gives excellent information about children who are gifted, along with suggestions for working with them.

The Indigo Children: The New Kids Have Arrived, by Lee Carroll and Jan Tober (Carson, Calif.: Hay House, 1999). This intriguing book describes the amazing attributes of the new children of the indigo color.

Second Branch: Compassion, Belonging, and Connection

Movies
It's A Wonderful Life. This inspiring spiritual film, directed by Frank Capra, powerfully illustrates the worth of a single human life and the importance of community.

Pay It Forward. This stirring movie portrays the power of good deeds.

Secret of Nimh. A field mouse seeks the aid of a colony of super-intelligent rats in order to save her son who is struggling with an illness. She discovers that she has a deeper link to them than she ever would have assumed.

Websites
Peace People. This organization was founded by Corrigan Maguire, a Catholic, and Betty Williams, a Protestant, as well as newspaper reporter Ciaran McKeown, to inspire global nonviolence. *www.peacepeople.com/MaireadCMaguire.htm*

The Daniel Pearl Foundation. This organization formed in memory of journalist Daniel Pearl to further the ideals that inspired Daniel's

life and work: promotion of cross-cultural understanding through journalism, music, and innovative communications.
www.danielpearl.org

The Beloved Community, by James Twyman, 1986. This is a rich resource of peace prayers set to music and drawn from the twelve major religions of the world: Hindu, Buddhist, Zoroastrian, Jainist, Jewish, Shinto, Native African, Native American, Muslim, Baha'i, Sikh, and Christian. James has performed the prayers around the world to tens of thousands of people.
www.emissaryoflight.com

The Ring. This peace network community, dedicated to the Native Americans of all nations, is a forum for uniting and sharing with the world their views, teachings, religions, and spirituality.
b.webring.com/hub?ring=natam

Books
I Can Show You I Care, by Susan Cotta (Berkeley, Calif.: North Atlantic Books, 2003). This useful introduction to receiving and giving hands-on healing shows how children were empowered by adopting safe compassionate touch along with simple acts of kindness.

Architects of Peace: Visions of Hope in Words and Images, by Michael Collopy (Novato, Calif.: New World Library, 2000). Seventy-five of the world's greatest peacemakers—spiritual leaders, politicians, scientists, artists, and activists—are featured as they testify to the wonderful diversity within humanity as well as unbelievable potential.

Eternal Echoes: Celtic Reflections on Our Yearning to Belong, by John O'Donohue (New York: HarperCollins, 2000). This book is poetic and speculative about the hunger to belong, and it explores the creative tension between eternal longing and belonging.

The Words of Peace: Selections from the Speeches of the Winners of the Nobel Peace Prize, by Irwin Abrams (New York: Newmarket Press, 1995). As we find encouragement in these heroes' words of peace, we are given significant perspectives on faith and hope, the connections of humanity, the heartbreak of war, violence and nonviolence, human rights, politics and leadership, and peace.

I'd Rather Teach Peace, by Colman McCarthy (New York: Orbis Books, 2002). This book tells the story of McCarthy, twenty-eight years a syndicated columnist for *The Washington Post*, challenging his students while introducing creative peacemaking.

The Power of Nonviolence: Writings by Advocates of Peace, by Howard Zinn (Boston: Beacon Press, 2002). As you read this anthology about peace, America is at war on terrorism. Is there a better way?

Starbright: Meditations for Children, by Maureen Garth (San Francisco: HarperCollins, 1991). This book is a collection of simple visualizations that Garth created for her child as she grew older.

Children of the New Millennium: Children's Near-Death Experiences and the Evolution of Humankind, by P.M.H. Atwater (New York: Three Rivers Press, 1999). As usual, Atwater is on the cutting edge of near-death research in her fascinating book.

An Open Heart: Practicing Compassion in Everyday Life, by the Dalai Lama (New York: Little, Brown and Company, 2001). This book describes the mechanisms by which a selfish heart becomes a compassionate person.

The Te of Piglet, by Benjamin Hoff (New York: Penguin Books USA, 1992). Piglet is the perfect personification of Te, the Taoist term for virtue, which is attained through compassion, humility, and smallness.

Third Branch: Physical Death

Movies

Somewhere in Time. This love story that transcends all time is produced by Stephen Simon and stars Christopher Reeve and Jane Seymour.

Ghost. This spellbinding movie portrays the eternal life of the soul.

Maytime. This is a beautiful story of the everlasting love of "Twin Souls" that surpasses time and place, starring Nelson Eddy and Jeanette McDonald.

The Sixth Sense. A boy who sees dead people who don't know they're dead has the dubious gift of communicating with spirits. As his journey is frightening to him, he seeks the help of a disheartened child psychologist.

Healing Activities

Puppet Plays for Grieving Children, by Sharon Rugg (Marietta, Ga.: Rising Sun Center for Loss and Renewal, 2000). This is a healthy and creative way to aid kids who are working through loss by engaging them in play with puppets.

A Forever Angel, by Elaine Stillwell (Omaha, Nebr.: Centering Corporation, 2001). This includes instructions on designing angels in memory of your loved ones.

Books

I Know I Made It Happen, by Lynn Bennett Blackburn (Burnsville, N.C.: Compassion Books, 2005). This is a gentle book about feelings that gives kids support during tough times, such as the death of a loved one.

Tear Soup: A Recipe for Healing After Loss, by Pat Schwiebert and Chuck DeKlyen (Portland, Ore.: Grief Watch; 3rd rev. ed., 2005).

In this modern fable, one of the most popular grief resources available for children and adults, a woman who has suffered a dreadful loss cooks up a special soup of the ingredients of her grief process. She gives out a recipe of good advice for those who have suffered a loss or know someone who has suffered a loss.

The Next Place, by Warren Hanson (Minneapolis, Minn.: Waldman House Press, 1997). When we die, our "spirit"—the energy of our thoughts and minds—must go somewhere. Hanson does an excellent job of describing this most indescribable of places (one which he says may not exist at all, except as a state of being).

Hello from Heaven: After-Death Communication Confirms That Life and Love Are Eternal, by Bill and Judy Guggenheim (New York: Bantam Books, 1996.) This book shares heartening messages from those who keep the connection alive from a life beyond physical death.

Healing the Bereaved Child, by Alan D. Wolfelt, Ph.D. (Fort Collins, Colo: Companion Press, 1996). Dr. Wolfelt has written a comprehensive resource for adults to assist companion boys and girls in their grief journeys.

Death Is of Vital Importance, by Elisabeth Kübler-Ross (New York: Station Hill Press, 1995). These children's stories about death show the reader that many times a person knows they are dying. As a result they find ways to prepare themselves for it. This book leaves the young and old alike with a sense of harmony and ease.

Fourth Branch: A World of Spirit

Movies
Lost Horizon. This Frank Capra masterpiece shows the dream of Shangri-La, a Utopian society, along with the love of "Twin Souls."

Fairytale. This is an intriguing look into the world of fairies and magic, produced by Wendy Finerman, who also produced *Forrest Gump*.

Spirited Away. Chihiro, a ten-year-old girl, wanders into a mystifying town. She soon learns that it is the "other world" of gods and monsters, where humans are changed into animals and a witch rules. Can she successfully return to her own world?

Books

A Child's Book of Angels, by Joanna Crosse (New York: Barefoot, 2000). This book is an introduction to angels, including the different types, how to recognize them, and how they help with dying or suffering people.

A Book of Angels, by Sophy Burnham (New York: Ballantine Books, 1990). These are extraordinary accounts of contemporary encounters with angels, as well as the study of angels through the ages and cultures.

Managing the Social and Emotional Needs of the Gifted: A Teacher's Survival Guide, by Connie C. Schmitz and Judy Galbraith (Minneapolis, Minn.: Free Spirit Publishing, 1985). Characteristics of gifted children are described in addition to gifted students' emotional and social needs.

Developing Students' Multiple Intelligences, by Howard Gardner (Jefferson City, Mo.: Scholastic, 1998). Howard Gardner states that the purpose of learning about multiple intelligences (MI) is to respect the many differences between people.

Talking to Heaven: A Medium's Message of Life after Death, by James Van Praagh (New York: Dutton, 1997). The author benefits from an amazing gift of communicating with the spirits of men, women, children, and animals who have died as he bridges the gap between the worlds of the physical and spiritual.

The Soul of the Child, by Michael Gurian (New York: Atria Books, 2002). Gurian focuses on the spiritual nature of children, encouraging parents to tend to their souls.

The Secret Spiritual World of Children, by Tobin Hart, Ph.D. (Makawao, Maui, Hawaii: Inner Ocean, 2003). Dr. Hart reveals many of the intricacies of a child's spiritual world that are kept secret, despite the fact that these secrets are enriching resources for boys' and girls' lives.

Fifth Branch: Light and Darkness, Good and Evil

Movies

The Godfather. The aging patriarch of an organized-crime family reassigns control of his covert operations to his reluctant son.

The Lord of the Rings: The Return of the King. Director Peter Jackson's generous, intelligent, and engrossing trilogy embraces Tolkien's world.

Books

People of the Lie, by M. Scott Peck (New York: Simon & Schuster, First Touchstone Edition, 1985; Second Touchstone Edition, 1998). Brilliantly probing the essence of human evil, the darker side of our existence, in this groundbreaking book Dr. Peck offers hope for triumphing over evil through confrontation and Christian love.

Glimpses of the Devil: A Psychiatrist's Personal Accounts of Possession, Exorcism, and Redemption, by M. Scott Peck (New York: Simon & Schuster, Free Press, 2005). Peck expands upon his beliefs in demonic possession after being a skeptic for most of his life about the existence of the devil. He gives readers the complete story of two clinical cases that made him a believer as well as an exorcist.

Prisoners of Hate, by Aaron Beck (New York: HarperCollins, 1999). This book offers remedies for dysfunctional thinking that results in acts anywhere from verbal abuse on the personal level to mass murder on the societal level.

Anger, Madness, and the Daimonic: The Psychological Genesis of Violence, Evil, and Creativity, by S. A. Diamond (Albany, N.Y.: State University of New York Press, 1996). Evil is an existential certainty, an unavoidable fact with which we humans must deal. The greatest evils we have to contend with today are hostility, hatred, and violence.

Way of the Peaceful Warrior, by Dan Millman (Tiburon, Calif.: H.J. Kramer, 1984). This book is one of the most dearly loved spiritual sagas of our time, dealing with light and shadow toward a final confrontation.

The Social Psychology of Good and Evil, by Arthur G. Miller (New York: Guilford Press, 2004). In this scholarly, state-of-the-art guidebook for our time, an all-star team of social psychologists explores the roots of the qualities of integrity, empathy, and self-sacrificial altruism as contrasted with hate, terrorism, and self-gratifying greed.

Evil: Inside Human Violence and Cruelty, by Roy F. Baumeister (New York: Owl Books, 1999). This book is a fascinating study of the roots of evil behavior from egotism and revenge to misplaced idealism and sadism.

Closer to the Light: Learning from the Near-Death Experiences of Children, by Melvin Morse, M.D. (New York: First Ballantine Books, 1991). This book is a compilation of amazing stories of what it feels like to die.

Embraced by the Light, by Betty J. Eadie (Placerville, Calif.: Gold Leaf Press, 1992). Eadie's account of dying in a hospital after surgery is one of the most profound near-death experiences ever.

The New Children and Near Death Experiences, by P.M.H. Atwater (Rochester, Vt.: Inner Traditions, 2003). Atwater provides an exceptionally comprehensive synopsis of the large variety of near-death experiences for children and how these transform their lives.

Sixth Branch: Healing Play

Movies

Lion King. Young lion Simba grieves the death of his father as his power-hungry uncle Scar causes him to leave the kingdom in shame. He eventually returns to take over for his father, King Mufasa, reclaiming his rightful place.

Pagemaster. By discovering a love for books in this animated fantasy adventure, a young boy confronts his phobias and learns to face life more courageously.

Books

Man and His Symbols, by Carl Jung (New York: Dell, 1968). Jung explores the world of the unconscious, whose language he thought to be the symbols of which dreams are made.

Play Therapy, by Virginia Axline (New York: Ballantine Books, 1947). A practical book taken from case histories gives specific illustrations of how to implement play therapy and also demonstrates how to effectively use the playroom toys.

Dibs in Search of Self, by Virginia Axline (New York: Ballantine Books, 1964). The author describes the intriguing journey of a young boy reaching for life through play therapy.

Windows to Our Children, by Violet Oaklander (New York: The Gestalt Journal Press, 1988). Using transcripts and case examples, methods, materials, and techniques for working with children and adolescents are concisely presented in this book.

Reaching Children Through Play Therapy: An Experiential Approach, by Carol Crowell Norton and Byron E. Norton (Denver, Colo.: White Apple Press, 2002). This book, a must-have for every play therapist's library (as well as for anyone interested in the welfare of children), very skillfully presents the brilliant method of play therapy the Nortons have used and taught for years.

The Healing Power of Play: Working with Abused Children, by Eliana Gil (New York: The Guilford Press, 1991). This book illustrates the tools needed for play therapy with abused children by giving clinical examples.

Therapeutic Metaphors for Children, by Joyce Mills and Richard Crowley (New York: Brunner/Mazel, 1986). The authors have applied the spirit of novelty and exploration natural to Milton Erickson's use of stories and metaphors to an exciting innovative arena of child therapy.

My Voice Will Go with You: The Teaching Tales of Milton H. Erickson, M.D., edited by Sydney Rosen (New York: W.W. Norton, 1991). Closely related to Milton Erickson's therapy was his use of "teaching tales." Dr. Rosen gathered together these tales in which Erickson called upon shock, surprise, and confusion, using questions, puns, and playful humor to seed suggestions.

Handbook of Play Therapy, by Charles Schaefer and K. J. O'Connor (New York: John Wiley and Sons, 1983). This book is a compilation of approaches to play therapy.

Seventh Branch: Transformation

Movies

Star Wars. George Lucas's first *Star Wars* film is the classic story of the Hero's Journey, a spiritual journey we are called to take to reach our spiritual potential. Joseph Campbell's *The Power of Myth* inspired Lucas's creation of this masterpiece.

My Life. This tremendous story starring Michael Keaton is one of personal growth and transcendence.

Fly Away Home. This movie is an engaging, enlightening example of the Hero's Journey for younger students.

Legend. This highly recommended older film teaches archetypes, symbols, and the Hero's Journey.

Books

The Dark Night of the Soul: A Psychiatrist Explores the Connection between Darkness and Spiritual Growth, by Gerald G. May, M.D. (New York: HarperCollins, 2004). Dr. May summarizes the writings of St. John of the Cross and St. Teresa of Avila, utilizing his psychological background to clarify the concept of the dark night of the soul.

When Bad Things Happen to Good People, by Harold S. Kushner (New York: Schocken Books, 1981). Kushner wrote this book as a reaction to personal tragedy—the death of his son Aaron, who suffered from premature aging.

Markings, by Dag Hammarskjold (New York: Knopf, 1966). This manuscript reflects a period of constant spiritual growth, self-questioning, and resolution.

Ladder of Perfection, by Walter Hilton, translated by Leo Sherley-Price (London and New York: Penguin, 1957, 1998). This work, written in 1494, is a guidebook for a spiritual journey through the mystical dark night.

The Collected Works of St. Teresa of Avila, Volume 1, translated by Kieran Kavanaugh and Otilio Rodriguez (Washington, D.C.: Institute of Carmelite Studies,1976). This book contains stories of St. Teresa's life, spiritual testimonies, and soliloquies, as well as a general and biblical index.

The Ecstatic Journey: The Transforming Power of Mystical Experience, by Sophy Burnham (New York: Ballantine Books,

1997). This book on mystical experiences contains interesting bits and pieces from the lives of the great mystics as well as very ordinary persons.

The Stormy Search for the Self, by Stan and Christina Grof (Los Angeles: J.P. Tarcher, 1991). With spiritual growth, intensely painful states of consciousness usually precede those of understanding and hope. Logic is not enjoyed, while intuition, inspiration, and imagination take precedence. Ego death is imminent.

The Power of Myth, by Joseph Campbell and Bill Moyers, edited by Betty Sue Flowers (New York: Doubleday, 1988). This companion book for *The Power of Myth*, a six-part miniseries first broadcast on PBS in 1988 (a year after Campbell's death) with Joseph Campbell and Bill Moyers, shows how we function to create and implement the themes of mythology.

Quest for the Crystal Castle, by Dan Millman (Tiburon, Calif.: H.J. Kramer, Starseed Press, 1992). Young Danny makes a "heroes journey" through an enchanted forest as he overcomes life's obstacles.

Magazines, Newspapers, Websites, and Associations

Sojourners Magazine, 3333 14th Street NW, Suite 200, Washington, D.C. 20010; (202) 328-8842. Sojourners is a Christian ministry whose mission is to join together spiritual renewal and social justice. *www.sojo.net*

Mothering, P.O. Box 1690, Santa Fe, N.M. 87504; 1-800-424-3308. This quarterly journal is full of fantastic parenting support.

Ave Maria Press, P.O. Box 428, Notre Dame, Ind. 46556-0428. The Press houses Spiritual Book Associates, a book club that provides direction to anyone's spiritual journey. *www.avemariapress.com*

ARE (Association for Research and Enlightenment, Inc.), Charles Thomas Cayce, 215 6th Street, Virginia Beach, Va. 23451-2061; (757) 428-3588. ARE was founded by Edgar Cayce to research matters such as holistic health, ancient mysteries, personal spirituality, dreams and dream interpretation, intuition, and philosophy and reincarnation. A global network of persons, this community offers conferences, educational events, and fellowship throughout the world.

APT (Association for Play Therapy, Inc.), 2060 N. Winery Ave., Suite 102, Fresno, Calif. 93703; (559) 252-2278; fax (559) 252-2297. APT provides a national list of play therapists.
www.a4pt.org

CAPT (Colorado Association of Play Therapy), 333 W. Drake Road, Suite 141, Fort Collins, Colo. 80526; (970) 484-6866. CAPT provides a list of play therapists in Colorado.
www.coloradoapt.org

Child/Spirit Institute, 35 Camp Court, Carrollton, Ga. 30117; (678) 839-0609. Tobin and Mary Hart's organization provides support, leadership, scholarship, and partnership for those involved in the emerging field of children's spirituality, while encouraging the natural capacity for wisdom, wonder, compassion, creativity, and questioning in both young people and adults.
www.childspirit.net

ISSSEEM (International Society for the Study of Subtle Energies and Energy Medicine), 11005 Ralston Road, Suite 210, Arvada, Colo. (303) 425-4625. This organization offers supportive contact through conferences for anyone interested in the field, while it acts as a bridge builder between communities and a leader in the exploration of consciousness, healing, and human potential.
www.issseem.org

ACEP (Association for Comprehensive Energy Psychology). ACEP offers supportive contact through conferences for professionals as it promotes collaboration among practitioners, researchers, and licensing bodies.

www.energypsych.org

Hospice Web—A Special Kind of Caring. This group provides information about hospice services in addition to a national directory of hospices. The more than 2,500 hospices in the United States provide social and spiritual support for the dying person and his or her family, including relief from pain for the patient.

www.hospiceweb.com

Index

comfort
  compassion, belonging,
    connection and, 30
  healing play and, 92–93
  light and darkness, good and
    evil and, 75
  physical death and, 45
  transformation and, 107
  wisdom and intuition and, 13
  a world of spirit and, 60
communication
  about spiritual companions,
    48, 58–59
  compassion, belonging
    connection and, 30
  creative expression and, 27,
    41, 46
  of dreams, 105, 107, 110
  of guilt, 11, 28, 82
  healing play and, 93
  light and darkness, good and
    evil and, 75
  physical death and, 46
  with spirits, xxi, xxvii
  with spiritual companions,
    49–55, 113
  transformation and, 107
  wisdom and intuition and, 13
  a world of spirit and, 60–61
  See also drawing as therapy;
    metaphor; stories
compassion, 15–30
  connection and, xxvii, 17,
    25–26, 30–31, 97, 106
  expression of, 25–26, 36,
    40, 99

family and, 19–20, 38, 99
compassionate connection, 17,
  25–26, 30–31, 106
confirmation
  compassion, belonging,
    connection and, 30
  healing play and, 92
  light and darkness, good and
    evil and, 74
  physical death and, 45
  transformation and, 106
  wisdom and intuition
    and, 12
  a world of spirit and, 60
conflict
  divorce and, 64–65, 91, 93
  internal, 44, 70, 88, 96,
    100–103
connection, 15–30, 25–26,
  31, 106
Connolly, John, xxi
creative expression
  communication and, 27, 41, 46
  potential for, xxiii, 30, 60,
    95, 111
  See also drawing as therapy

death
  desire for, 16, 67
  discussion of, 2, 42–46
  of extended family members,
    7–9, 48–50, 90
  fear of, 2, 9, 28, 44, 86,
    103–4
  grief and, xiii, 2, 7–8, 29,
    31–33, 83–85

teachers, 59, 60, 70, 72, 111

therapeutic play. *See* healing play

therapeutic playroom. *See* healing play

therapists, 45, 60, 74, 92, 106, 115

therapy, xxvii–xxxi, 92

touch, appropriate, 12

transformation, 95–107
  healing play and, 37–38, 82
  metaphor and, xxix–xxx, 78
  prayer and, 65

trauma, xxvii, 6, 78

Tree of Life, xxv

trust, 114–16
  issues with, xxx, 8, 29, 32
  safety and, 66–69, 110
  spiritual partners and, xix, 73, 110–14

truth telling, 35, 39, 98–99

unconditional love, xxxi, 20–21, 74

validation
  of feelings, 45, 110
  of spiritual capacity, 11, 13
  of spiritual companions, xxi, 58–61, 117

Virgin Mary, 51
  visions, xiii, xiv, 55–56. *See also* dreams

Western mind, xxi

wisdom
  innate, xiii, xxi–xxiv, 4, 6, 77
  metaphor and, 86
  spiritual, 1–13, 97, 101
  support of, 105

writing
  anger expression and, 33
  as creative expression, 27–28
  journal writing, 11–12, 60, 73
  of letters, 37, 105